POWER FLOWER

AKA

INDIGO SWAN

By Anthea A Jones

Original Copyright Anthea A Jones 2018
All rights reserved.
ISBN 9781795419482

Contents

Introduction	4
Growing in the Dark	7
Beginning to Change	19
Growing in the Light	24
Scriptures from The Aquarian Gospel of Jesus the Christ by Levi	53
Hands-on-Healing Testimonials	102

Introduction.

The Aquarian Gospel of Jesus the Christ by Levi is a rock for me, hence its inclusion. Here is some of what I love about this book:-

- Scriptures from the Akashic Records, where every thought, word and deed is recorded on the Spiritual Plane.
- Jesus speaking highly of the original pure sacred teachings of the Avesta, the Vedas, Tao Great, the Psalms, the Prophets, Gautama and more before they were changed.
- Life and Works of Jesus in India, Tibet, Persia, Assyria, Greece and Egypt.
- Education of Mary and Elizabeth in Zoan.
- The Truth of the Brotherhood of man. We are all One.
- Explanations such as:

1.   Christ means Love.

68:11 to 13 The Aquarian Gospel of Jesus the Christ by Levi.

11. Men call me Christ, and God has recognized the name; but Christ is not a man. The Christ is universal love, and Love is king.

12. This Jesus is but man who has been fitted by temptations overcome, by trials multiform, to be the temple through which Christ can manifest to men.

13. Then hear, you men of Israel, hear! Look not upon the flesh; it is not king. Look to the Christ within, who shall be formed in every one of you, as he is formed in me.

2. The Ages.

LEVI'S COMMISSION. [Extract. Full in Chapter of Scriptures.] The Aquarian Gospel of Jesus the Christ by Levi.

This age will be an age of splendor and of light, because it is the home age of the Holy Breath; and Holy Breath will testify anew for Christ, the Logos of eternal Love.

At first of every age this Logos is made manifest in flesh so man can see and know and comprehend a Love that is not narrow, circumscribed.

Twelve times in every revolution of the sun this christed Love of God is made full manifest in flesh upon the planes of earth, and you may read in Akasha the wondrous lessons that these Christs have taught to men; but you shall publish not to men the lessons of the Christs of ancient times.

Now, Levi, message bearer of the Spirit Age, take up your pen and write.

Write full the story of the Christ who ...... men have known as Enoch the Initiate.

And you may write the story of Melchizedec, the Christ who lived when Abram lived, ...

And you may write the story of the Prince of Peace, the Christ who came as babe in Bethlehem, ...

157:29 The Aquarian Gospel of Jesus the Christ by Levi.

29. And then the man who bears the pitcher will walk forth across an arc of heaven; the sign and signet of the son of man will stand forth in the eastern sky.

In other words Jesus and the Christs before Him e.g., Enoch and Melchizedec plus those to come in future ages are the Master Souls who perfected Love. Hence them being glorified. The Master Soul of this age is Jesus, of the Aquarian age, born in the Piscean age.

Growing in the Dark.

I was born on the 31st of August 1966 in Cyprus. The parents, I will call Jane and Richard (names are changed), were living there at the time, as Richard who was in the RAF had been posted there.
I only spent the first 6 months of my life in Cyprus, so I do not remember it. My childhood was in England, Middlesex; Stanmore and Harrow. My brother was born in 1971.

Primary school, middle school and secondary school were for me mostly unhappy and painful, specifically because of the overt racism towards people of African ancestry during the 60s and 70s in England.

I remember during one morning assembly at primary school, whilst singing a hymn, I suddenly found myself unable to breathe. I was taken out into the hallway. We were singing words about joy and happiness but I could not sing them because it was the opposite to how I felt. I later learnt that it was a panic attack. In the playground at primary school, we would hold hands and sing as we skipped around in a circle; "Eenie meanie miny mo, catch a nigger by its toe..."

At play time in middle school we would play British bulldog. You would line up, and then try to run from one end of the playground to the other whilst two children tried to stop you. It was a rough game. Initially I was the only child of African ancestry amongst my peers at my middle school. I was more often tackled and more harshly so, than my Caucasian peers. I really hated that game but each time I played it, I hoped, though it was always in vain, it would not be a painful experience.

In 1977 when I was 11 years old, Roots was shown on TV. Although it was difficult to watch, what I found more painful was being on the receiving end of the taunting about it, from some of my secondary school Caucasian peers.

The home life was dominated by domestic violence. Richard would regularly physically assault Jane. I remember Jane wearing sunglasses to hide black eyes. I do not remember when the domestic violence started; it just always seemed to exist. It was a tense household. I remember when lying awake in bed, not yet having managed to fall asleep, on hearing Richard's keys opening the front door, I would feel anxious about what may happen that evening/night, be it arguments or physical violence. Although I did experience some physical punishment, it did not feel excessive, however the emotional violence in the form of Richard's tendency towards vulgar name-calling, as I grew into a teenager/young woman, was very upsetting. His want for control, prevented me from developing a typical healthy teenage/young woman social life. I felt unheard and so desperate to try to change things at home that in the midst of an argument, I slashed my arm with a bread knife. Things did not change for the better. Instead as I grew older, gradually my curfew became earlier.

I remember my careers interview at school. I was excited about it; however I left feeling without hope and the future seemed very grey. I believe it was indicative of the lack of expectation and support at the time, for people of African ancestry, be it children or adults.

I went to a sixth form college to take 'A' Levels. I chose 'A' Level French and Sociology plus an additional 'O' Level in Law. However my only real focus at college was freedom. I regularly missed lessons and instead either hung around in the common room or went into the Harrow town centre.

I had decided to take a teaching degree at university following my 'A' Levels, however I did not achieve the grades necessary; indicative of my lack of application to my studies.

I took a local administrative post and tried to embark on the start of my life as an official adult at the age of 18. Two weeks after my 18th birthday whilst out with friends in the evening, I rang home to try to extend the curfew time, I had been given. I spoke with Richard. He said no. I decided to stay overnight at a friend's house.

In the morning I returned home to get ready to go to work. When I entered my bedroom, I saw that my clothes having been taken out of the wardrobe were now on my bed. Richard came into my room with a belt in his hand. I was shocked when I saw it, as I assumed that now I was officially an adult, he would not hit me. When he moved towards me to strike me, I fell back onto the bed and I kicked him to prevent him from doing so. He still struck me with the belt and I cried for a while after but I knew then, I needed to leave home. I understood at that moment he now saw me as another adult female, that he had the right to physically assault.

I moved in with some friends of a friend and in the years that followed, I lived in various places; sometimes house sharing and other times not. For the majority of my working life, apart from three and a half years when I worked in advertising, I worked in roles that were to support different groups of people to overcome their challenges. I mostly worked with young people who were struggling and at risk of being excluded from school and/or offending, as well as working with their parents/carers.

I very much wanted to help people because of the suffering that I had gone through, however I was still struggling myself. There were another three incidents of self-harm, two taking an overdose of tablets and one using a knife to cut my wrist. In 1993 I began to smoke marijuana on a daily basis; sometimes I smoked skunk. I tried to stop smoking these drugs but whenever I did I ended up smoking cigarettes/rolled up tobacco and/or drinking excessive amounts of alcohol.

As I had not learnt how to develop healthy relationships, this had a negative impact on my ability to understand what healthy relationships should feel like. I had instead learnt how to tolerate abusive relationships.

During a mild disagreement with a boyfriend at the time, at the point when I found my voice - this was later explained by the Relate counsellor - he got up from the sofa he was sitting on and came across to the sofa I was sitting on. I thought he was coming to hug me but instead he sat on me, facing me and held me down as he spoke aggressively to me. I was shocked and initially froze. I then became very distressed. He then got off me. I ran off into my bedroom and cried. I then found my voice again and told him to leave my home. I could not understand exactly how to see what had happened. I was angry and I was sad but I was confused as to whether I should stay with him or end the relationship. The Relate counsellor wanted us to come back for more sessions, however when I heard him speak dismissively of her afterwards, I knew that going back to counselling sessions was not the answer. One day I went to try to describe how I felt on paper and a poem came. It spoke of muddy hands and self-imposed shackles. Only years later, did I realise it had come from Spirit/God. I contacted the National Domestic Violence Helpline plus read thoroughly again and again the advice on their website on how to identify domestic violence; to see whether a perpetrator of domestic violence was truly remorseful and if their mind was set to change. I saw evidence of the opposite of the latter. I ended the relationship. I later understood that the self-imposed shackles referred to the fact that I had chosen to stay in a relationship with someone, who had already shown me much unkindness.

One day a few years later, having been in discussion with someone who was then a former boyfriend, about the possibility of us resuming the relationship, I decided to go to his home to talk further about this. He was not expecting me and was not happy that I had arrived without us having arranged this prior but in particular, he was not happy because unknown to me, he now had a removable false tooth, which he had not put in before opening the door. When he spoke and I saw the gap of the missing tooth, immediately a thought came into my head which was about karma. I thought "someone also punched you in the face, as you punched me in the face." I was taken aback by this thought and I could not make sense of it at the time. I did not speak to him about it. He put the tooth in and we talked. This thought however came back into my mind as I drove home and I realised it was referring to an incident that had taken place in a karate class; I had attended some time before. I had begun to take karate lessons at the karate club he attended. One day when we were sparring he punched me in the face. I was completely shocked, though what disturbed me more were the reactions from others in the class which included some of his friends, who had witnessed this. On speaking to them after, I learnt that they knew as he was a black belt and I had not even begun to grade, so was a white belt, he did this on purpose. He denied this and said it was an accident. Although I was upset about it, I allowed it to go to the back of my mind and the relationship continued. Before and after this incident, I had ended the relationship several times (and allowed it to resume) because of sensing a coldness from him but until this day of going to his home and having the karmic thought, I had never faced what he really did to me that day in the karate class. After I had understood the meaning of this karmic thought, which I realised years later was from Spirit/God, now having arrived home, I phoned him and confronted him about this. I expected him this time to admit what he had done and to sincerely apologise. However he told me that he never wanted to speak to me again. I understood that this was because he knew, I now saw clearly that he had chosen to punch me in the face, that day in the karate class. Years later I bumped into an old friend who also knew him and I told her about this last communication with him. She told me that he had also punched in the face another mutual female friend of ours, who had been attending the same karate club. She was a lower grade in karate than him and she had been sparring with him at the time.

The relationship of Jane and Richard continued until the early 1990s. They had planned to return to live in the Caribbean. Richard went earlier to take up a job and Jane stayed in England to sell the house; set to join him after. I did not understand why Jane, having been on the receiving end of so much physical violence from Richard, would want to leave England to go to live with him in a small Caribbean island, particularly as it was the island that he was from; not the island she was from, thereby leaving her without easy access to her family or friends for support. Whilst Jane was in England and Richard was in the Caribbean they communicated by phone, as well as letter. I do not know all that transpired in their communication, however shortly before Jane was set to go to the Caribbean, having sold the house, she received a letter from Richard which she showed to me. In this letter Richard told Jane that he did not want her to come to the Caribbean to live with him. They eventually divorced. Jane continued to live in England and Richard continued to live in the

Caribbean. They both had subsequent relationships and Jane remarried.

I saw that Jane's husband, who was Caucasian, would frequently make racist remarks. Sometimes he would laugh when making these remarks; his comments were similar to the content of the now banned racist comedies of the 1970s. Other times he would try to bring the focus of conversation to events/times when people of African ancestry were disempowered e.g., the transatlantic slave trade. When I would try to turn the focus of these latter conversations, to examples of people of African ancestry being empowered, he became disinterested in continuing the conversation. Jane sometimes would address his racist remarks but on the whole tolerated them.

In 2008, I attended a barbecue at the home of Jane and her husband. Present were also the boyfriend at that time and his mother, as I had invited them. He was the boyfriend who following his act of violence towards me in 2009, I had attended the Relate counselling session with. I was standing in the garden and suddenly Jane's husband slapped his hand across my bottom. I was so shocked; I could not believe what he had done. I froze inside and said nothing. Sometime after the boyfriend spoke of this. He said that both he and his mother had seen what Jane's husband had done to me. I would not engage in the conversation. I could not bear to think about it, let alone talk about it.

In 2011, I attended the funeral of an uncle. I was standing in the cemetery during the burial. Jane and her husband were standing behind me. My brother was standing to my right. All of a sudden Jane's husband pulled me into him by putting his right arm around my waist. As it was unexpected I fell back into him - there was no gap between the back of my body and the front of his. I was so shocked. I once again froze inside, moved away from him and said nothing.

In 2011, I went to see The Lion King with Jane and her husband. I travelled separately and met them outside of the theatre. I arrived first. When they arrived Jane told me that her husband had touched a woman on her leg, as he was speaking to the woman on the train, on the way to the theatre. When I spoke to Jane's husband about this, he laughed dismissively. I spoke to him of the disrespect he had caused Jane and said that the woman, who he had touched on the train, would have been aware of what he had done to her. I still however had not spoken to him, about his inappropriate touching of me.

The relationship with Richard continued to be difficult. I went to the Caribbean to visit him, as well as to spend time with my stepsister who was now born and he stayed with me once when he came to England. I believed our relationship was repairing but it was still broken. This was evident by his tendency to still be cold.

Beginning to Change.

In March 2011, I left the local authority that I was working for to become self-employed. Redundancies were being made. In the department that I worked for, four positions were going to become three. I strongly felt the need to become self-employed; I wanted to feel empowered, so I applied for voluntary redundancy. However I also applied for one of the three positions. I did not get one of these three positions and I was very upset, even though my heart was set on becoming self-employed. I cried daily for about a week after learning that I had not got one of these positions. Once I began to look at the possibilities of my future as a self-employed Parenting Worker, I realised that the feeling of being upset before was because I had struggled to let go.

I started to walk and cycle along the Grand Union Canal. I began to frequently visit local parks and the London parks. I loved feeding the ducks and swans, the views of the trees and watching the other wildlife. One day as I was walking along the Grand Union Canal, I had a vision of a newborn baby with brown skin and cradle cap on its head. It was like a photo had been put in front of me. I wondered who the baby was. I had never had a vision like this before. I later learnt that it was showing, I was going to be reborn.

I joined a steel pan band. I had no experience of playing steel pan before but I really enjoyed learning and playing. I made new friends and played at the Notting Hill Carnival. There were however a minority of men who would try to touch women, when there was no invitation to do so or there was a clear indication that their advances were not welcome. In the first year, I experienced this with three men who did touch me inappropriately, however this time when it occurred with each of these three men, I spoke out loudly and clearly. I confronted each one of them after their act of assault and told them that unless they showed me true remorse for what they had done, I would not speak to them. They did not show remorse for what they had done, though they would try to disregard what they had done and talk to me. I would not allow what they had done to me, to be disregarded and therefore I did not speak to them. I played with the band for a total of four years.

I began to read a book that had contributions from various people, speaking about positive thinking.

One of these people had a spiritual centre in America and had a conference coming up in England. I went to the conference and I really enjoyed it.

I registered at a new local dentist. As he was of African ancestry, in particular born in an African country, I spoke to him about my interest in tracing back my ancestors, to beyond the Caribbean. He gave me some pointers to help me with my research.

The Christmas of 2011 was approaching and having been able to see the difference of how I felt since March 2011, I decided not to spend Christmas Day with Jane and her husband.

I began to read the material and live stream the services of the spiritual centre in America whose conference I had attended. I also watched the live streaming of one of their Christmas/New Year celebrations. I was amazed at how happy they seemed, dancing to house music - which I particularly enjoy - with spiritual words because (as far as I could see) there was an absence of alcohol/drugs. I wanted to be a part of their community. I wanted to move there and train to become one of their spiritual practitioners.

On 28th March 2012, I finally stopped smoking marijuana and skunk. There were various factors that helped. The person I bought it from was going to emigrate in May 2012 and I did not want to start buying it from someone that I did not know, having gone to the same person for many years. I also did not want to feel desperate, when I could no longer buy it from him. I no longer believed in my own justifications for smoking marijuana nor skunk which included: they were herbs; they were for self-medication; they were alternatives to Prozac; they were alternatives to alcohol. However the biggest motivation for stopping smoking marijuana and skunk was my son, who was approaching the age of 18. I wanted to be a good example. I did not want, not to be in a position to advise him against the consequences of depending on it. I had my son in 1994 and although his father, who is Caucasian, was a very kind man, I was not emotionally developed enough to sustain a healthy relationship. Gratefully he is a wonderful father and is happily remarried. One of the ways that I helped myself to stop smoking marijuana and skunk, was to place a collection of CDs of the sounds of nature e.g., birds singing, on my coffee table in my bedroom, so if I struggled to sleep at night I could easily reach them. I found though that I did not play them often. I also took long walks in nature which helped. However to my amazement, it was not as hard as I had expected to stop smoking marijuana and skunk. I later understood that because I had asserted my own will, I received additional help from Spirit/God.

On the 5th April 2012, I felt inspired to stop drinking alcohol for Lent. It only occurred to me a couple of days later into Lent, that as I had also stopped smoking marijuana and skunk, I had no alcohol/substances to lean on. I was surprised I did not see this before making a commitment, to stop drinking alcohol for Lent. One day I attended a small theatre production and took a seat at the front. The person sitting next to me had a pint of beer. Unexpectedly, I found the smell of the beer turned my stomach. Much to my surprise, when Lent had ended, I found that I had no desire to drink alcohol again. I was very grateful because I now knew I would not end up depending on drinking excessive amounts of alcohol, to replace the marijuana and skunk, as well as the cigarettes/rolled up tobacco that I had now given up.

Growing in the Light.

On the 28th April 2012, after I woke up, I sat up in my bed to meditate. I said I wanted to do something with my hands. I had no idea what I meant. I went to yoga later that morning and afterwards I shared this with one of the women in the class. I was surprised I had spoken to her about this because although we had chatted before I did not know her that well. She began to tell me about hands-on-healing, which I did not know about and that she had attended hands-on-healing courses, one of which she recommended. Later that evening I decided to do some research about hands-on-healing on the internet and I began printing out lots of articles. However my printer became jammed. At that time a thought came into my head - that I had not decided to do hands-on-healing but it had come from within, so I should let it continue to unfold in that way.

Over the following 10 days, as I had gained this understanding - that I was a channel through which healing would happen and that I was not the one doing the healing but by placing my hand on a person, healing would take place; I asked Jane if I could try this out on her. The first time she fell into a very sleepy state. I was amazed. The second time, she seemed to be closed. I noticed that her hands were clasped together across her lap, as opposed to the first time when her arms were hanging loosely by her side and I shared my observation with her, suggesting that she tried to relax more but she defended how she was. This surprised me, as I thought that she would have been glad, I had pointed this out. As she was leaving my house, I asked her how she felt during the session. She said she had felt pressure in her forehead. I was amazed to hear this, though also surprised that she did not share this with me after the session, as she knew I was trying to gain more understanding about this new gift of hands-on-healing, I had received.

In early May, I received the name of this spiritual healing service from Spirit/God - Indigo Swan Hands-on-Healing. I could understand why "Swan" was in the name, as I had really been enjoying swans on my trips along the canal. I also had a particularly special experience with the swans. One time before April 2012, as I was watching them on the canal waters, I wondered if they could fly because of their size and I related this to how I was feeling - could I fly, could I feel light, as I felt so heavy. I remember researching on the internet whether or not swans could fly. I saw they could. A couple of days later, as I was again walking along the canal, two swans took off and flew, then landed again on the canal waters. It was a beautiful moment which I treasured. I initially did not understand why "Indigo" was in the name. I later learnt it was an anagram for God in I.

I began to create flyers for this spiritual healing service. I placed them in libraries, hospitals and community organisations. I also placed them in the branches of a wholefood/natural products store, which at the time had local alternative practitioners in their branches on a rotational basis, promoting their services.

Initially I thought 40 minutes was the length of time needed to deliver the spiritual healing and so when in January 2014 I was inspired to deliver 5 minute sessions, I first saw them as tasters, however I later learnt 5 minutes was all that was needed. I was amazed as I observed the healing that was taking place through me - emotional healing, physical healing, inspiration and enlightenment. Testimonials are included at the back of this book. I knew that Jesus was carrying out the healing through me. On the 11th August 2012, as I awoke He said to me "I want to heal you and heal through you." I also learnt that He healed everyone irrespective of a person's religion/spiritual belief or sexual orientation. I remember a Muslim lady hearing the sound of gongs during her spiritual healing session. I thought how lovely that was created for her, as it was a sound familiar in her traditional religious practice. I remember being surprised when a different Muslim lady, who was with her three children, took a spiritual healing session in the busy thoroughfare of a shopping centre, in front of one of the branches of the wholefood/natural products store; I delivered spiritual healing at, specifically because she was wearing a burqa. It taught me not to make assumptions about who Jesus heals. I saw Him heal people who were Hindu, Sikh, Buddhist, Jewish, of other religions, generally spiritual and agnostic. I remember Jesus advised a gay man that his partner was not being honest with him. I had no ability to determine the outcome of the spiritual healing and I did not know what a person was experiencing unless they shared it with me.

In 2012, I went to my dentist. He asked me how my research into my ancestry was going. I told him where I got up to but I was actually no longer interested in pursuing this further, as I was now interested in pursuing my spirituality. He then informed me, he was also a part-time pastor. When I shared with him my experiences he told me that the main pastor of his church did not go to a theological college and was taught by Spirit/God direct. He told me that he believed I would develop a healing ministry. Over the years, I have continued to share with him my journey. I saw why he had really become my dentist. Spirit/God had sent me to him for support because he would be able to understand that Spirit/God was teaching me directly.

In June 2012, I bought an Aramaic version of the Bible. I read some of the Old Testament but focused on the New Testament and continued to read it from the beginning again, when I got to the end. I recognised the teaching in it "Love Your Neighbour As Yourself" in my observations of the healing that Jesus was carrying out through me. However I saw that some of the content of the Bible did not reflect the Divine Love that I observed in the healing that Jesus carried out through me nor did I sense in my spirit at times when reading the Bible, that Divine Love.

In July 2012, I now felt strong enough to tell Jane what her husband had done to me. My main concern though was how she would cope and I contacted my brother to ask him to support her. I was shocked by both of their responses. Jane's response was anger towards me. She tried to justify her anger by saying I was at fault because I had not told her sooner. I assumed this was just an initial reaction and that she would be devastated when she realised what her husband had done to me. My brother showed me no compassion either, so much so, that during the conversation when I asked him to support Jane, because of his coldness towards me, I said to him that unless he was able to feel warmth and compassion for me regarding this, I could no longer speak to him. His absence of warmth and compassion lasted for just under 6 years. In his communication to me on the 21st of June 2018 he wrote "I understand and accept that I didn't support you or show any compassion in the way a brother should." We are now moving forward.

In September 2012, I had six prophetic dreams that all showed me, as I had now spoken out about what Jane's husband had done to me, what was going to happen. I had never had prophetic dreams before. I did not understand them at the time but wrote them down. In one, I was going up and down a very narrow staircase. It was dark and I was distressed because I could not seem to get to the top. I eventually got to the top and saw the front room in the house of Jane and her husband. They were both sitting on the sofa with their arms folded. I later learnt that this was to show me, that Jane was not helpless and was choosing to stay in the relationship with her husband, in spite of knowing that he had inappropriately touched her daughter. In another prophetic dream, I was in a courtroom standing in the witness box, screaming to be heard, however in front of me all the seats were empty apart from a couple. I next found myself sitting in one of the seats at the edge of the courtroom. I looked up and saw Jane's husband standing next to me. I could not believe how he could stand there without any remorse, for what he had done to me. On the day of Jane's birthday in May 2013, I suddenly found myself driving to the home of Jane and her husband. I had not planned to do so. I did not notify them that I was coming. I could see after that Spirit/God had given me strength to do this. When I arrived I said to Jane, although it was her birthday I did not come to wish her happy birthday but that she would be grateful that I did what I had come to do. I walked into the front room and Jane's husband was sitting at the dining room table. I went and sat opposite him. I confronted him about what he had done to me. Jane sat on the arm of the sofa. I was amazed at the projection of my voice, as it was so strong. Neither during or after I had spoken about the two times he had touched me inappropriately, did he question me or deny this or apologise. He said nothing. I then turned to Jane and I spoke to her about a recurring dream that she had told me about. She had explained previously, in this dream she found herself alone in a house and when she opened the door she saw outside the sea was rising. She said she was afraid that it would come into the house. At the time when she had explained it, I had no idea what the dream was about. However at that moment, when I turned to her after having confronted her husband, I suddenly knew what I needed to say to her about the dream. I said that I was confused, as to why she kept opening the door, when she knew the sea was rising, as it could come into the house. After I had explained this to her, Jane's husband spoke for the first time, since I had confronted him. He began to try to dismiss what I had said. I later understood that Spirit/God had given me the understanding of her dream; that Jane had known for quite some time, that she was choosing to do what was wrong. After I had finished speaking to Jane about her dream, her husband went into the kitchen. I got up to leave and as I approached the front room door, I stopped for a moment in front of Jane. I said that she was in an emotionally abusive and violent relationship with Richard and now she was in an emotionally abusive relationship with her husband. At that point Jane's husband came rushing out of the kitchen and stood close at my right side to try to intimidate me, so I would stop speaking. I put my hand up to indicate I was not going to engage with him and without facing him, I told him not to come any closer. I understood later that the prophetic dream, in which he had stood next to me in the courtroom, was to show me that he was going to do what he did - stand at my side to try to intimidate me. The empty chairs in the courtroom showed the lack of support I would receive, for dealing with what Jane's husband had done to me, once I had spoken out about it. When I got into my car to drive home Jane came into the car for a while. I told her that at her barbecue, the boyfriend at the time and his mother were both witnesses of her husband's inappropriate touching of me. Sometime after she told me that she had called his mother to speak to her about this but his mother said she did not remember seeing this and spoke of not wanting to split up a family. I tried for a while to continue a relationship with Jane but I could not. I realised later that the six prophetic dreams and the understanding of Jane's dream that I had been given, were so I would know that I could never feel peace, if I continued to have a relationship with Jane.

In December 2013, a repossession order on my home was granted by the court. I had not been able to keep up with the mortgage payments. I was worried and confused as to why I had not been able to generate a sufficient income to pay for my financial commitments. As I approached my bed that night of the repossession order being granted, to go to sleep, I heard very gently the hymn "To Be a Pilgrim." Although I did not know what the future held, I felt comforted by this and I went to sleep. The next morning shortly after I woke up, I understood I was to take on lodgers. This would enable me to pay my mortgage. I proceeded quickly with making the arrangements to take on my first lodger. I continued to have lodgers until July 2017. On looking back, I was amazed to see there was one particular lesson that I kept learning again and again with each lodger. This lesson was the tendency to let things go. Although I had house rules, I would often not bring what was not followed immediately to the lodger's attention. I gradually learnt more and more, that as people choose to do what they want, if I did not speak out, I would always tolerate what I did not want. The biggest factor however that caused me to be apprehensive about confronting my lodgers was the fear of losing money. I worried that if I confronted them about the house rules they had not followed, they may have decided to leave. I accrued debts with most of my creditors including the council tax department and the housing association I paid rent to - the property being shared-ownership. I was constantly engaged in very distressing conversations about my inability to maintain my financial commitments with them. However in spite of this, I always had what I needed, though often I would not know very much in advance when I would receive the money to pay for food and other essential outgoings including utilities but Spirit/God always provided me with what I needed in time. I found out I had entitlement to different grants and benefits, both of which before leaving employment, I never would have expected to apply for.

By August 2014, Jesus had carried out just under 300 spiritual healing sessions through me. On the evening of Sunday 10th August 2014, I saw that I was to bring the hands-on-healing service to an end. I did not understand completely why at the time but because I thought I was to create a business out of the hands-on-healing and this had not manifested, it made sense. I had no idea what I was going to do instead. When I woke up the following morning I felt inspired to look into fitness instructor courses. I loved exercise and had been participating in various forms of exercise - aerobics, weight training, yoga, Pilates, African dancing, spinning/indoor cycling, swimming and outdoor cycling for over 20 years, so although this work was very different, I was really excited that this was the direction I was being led to take. I found a personal training course which really appealed to me. It included 'Pads for PTs' (personal trainers) and 'HIIT' (high intensity interval training). I was able to receive a student loan for the majority of the course fee but I also needed to put down a deposit to book the course. I took a three month temporary position in a customer services department to save up for this deposit and also for the money that I would need, when I began to study full-time.

In September 2014, I began to attend a traditional Christian church.

My personal training course began in January 2015 and ended in March 2015. I loved this course. It was exciting and invigorating.

My first job in the fitness industry was a gym instructor in a community leisure centre, which I started on the 27th April 2015. My two main shifts were to supervise the women-only gym sessions. Part of this role involved ensuring that men did not enter these women-only gym sessions. During the women-only gym sessions which took place in the smaller gym upstairs, men, as well as women who did not want to use the women-only gym sessions, used the main gym downstairs. Very often, although the women-only gym sessions were clearly indicated by women-only signs on the two doors plus additional signs next to the two door handles and one of the doors was kept locked, as well as the blinds pulled down, some men would persist in coming into the women-only gym sessions. I was very able to confront these men about clearly choosing to ignore that it was a women-only gym session and irrespective of how they tried to hide their dishonesty, I could still see it. I did not tolerate any disrespectful behaviour towards me or towards the women using the women-only gym sessions from these men.

On the 28th April 2015, I began to deliver youth gym sessions in the youth club that was run by the traditional Christian church that I attended, other traditional Christian churches in the local area, as well as the youth services department of that borough. There were young people of all different religions/spiritual beliefs. Although I enjoyed some parts of the regular Sunday church service, when there was a reference to people of other religions/spiritual beliefs in a negative way, I struggled. I knew that this representation of the teachings of Spirit/God/Jesus was not right. I had seen how He healed and loved all people irrespective of their religion/spiritual belief, whilst delivering spiritual healing through me. I was confused as to how the regular Sunday church services could speak in a negative way about people who were not identified as Christian, when in the youth club I saw love for all the young people, irrespective of their religion/spiritual belief. My struggle was compounded by the fact that the community leisure centre I worked at was in Hayes, an area of high Asian population.

The persistence of men trying to come into the women-only gym sessions continued. One Saturday morning after meditating, still sitting up in bed, I found myself writing a letter to the management team of the community leisure centre; asking them to take further action to address this. To my amazement in the letter I spoke of understanding that; for some of the Muslim women, exercising in the view of men was considered a sin against God. I remember sometime after I had written the letter, I asked myself how I knew this, as I had not researched this nor had any of the Muslim women explained this to me. I understood that Spirit/God had told me. I asked in the letter, if it could be clearly stated in the notices informing that a women-only gym session was taking place; that the consequences of men ignoring this rule would result in memberships being suspended. On the 31st August 2015, my birthday, I received confirmation that this action would be taken, as well as a copy of the new notice to be displayed. I saw it as a victory, particularly because receiving this confirmation on my birthday, highlighted this was work that Spirit/God/Jesus had given me to do. It also felt so great to be given work by Spirit/God/Jesus, to support people of another religion (at the time I identified myself as Christian); to be able to honour Spirit/God in the way that was right for them. I shared this victory with a senior member of the traditional Christian church I was attending. This was their reply: "Hey Anthea, Thanks for sharing this with me. You were brave and obedient to God. He is using you to bless people He loves and bring glory to Him. Well done and thanks for blessing me too by sharing your story with me. Happy birthday." I was very happy to receive their message and I hoped that this understanding of the uncircumscribed love of

Spirit/God/Jesus would filter down into the church.

One day I was asked if I would like to help out at the Sunday school of the traditional Christian church I was attending. I was definitely interested in helping out, though I knew that because of the big difference in belief held by myself and the traditional Christian churches, I needed to be clear to them on what I would say to children attending the Sunday school about my beliefs. That afternoon I began to write an email to the relevant church members, which included the minister. I was so nervous; my hands were shaking as I typed, specifically because I was challenging someone who had been a minister for over 20 years about the teachings of Spirit/God/Jesus. About 15 minutes into writing this email, I received a message via messenger from a friend who also attended this church but was over 4000 miles away on holiday and had no idea that I had been asked to help out at the Sunday school nor that I was writing this email at that moment. This was their message: "Hi I have been thinking about you and I feel I should say...Trust and surrender and listen to the voice in your heart (that is God)" I was amazed. I continued to write the email confidently. Lots of emails followed after the sending of my first email. The minister said that although I had explained to him, when I first began to attend the church, what I believed, he did not think I still thought that way. I realised then, that we both thought each other would change. One of the responses from someone else who attended the church, I realised much later included a prophecy of my future work as a spiritual healer: "I believe that God has a special call on your life." In September 2015, I left the traditional Christian church I had been attending.

My work as a fitness professional continued to develop. I began to take classes outdoors and indoors, including weight training, boot camp, total body workout, indoor cycling, keep fit 50 +, buggy exercise, back to exercise, box fit, as well as deliver personal training. I loved my work as a fitness professional. I enjoyed sharing with people what I had learnt about developing and maintaining physical fitness. I felt a lot of love from all the wonderful people I engaged with on this part of my journey. I also learnt to continue further developing a sense of self. As an independent personal trainer, I had to develop my own contracts and over time I saw how I needed to change the terms and conditions, so that they would be fair for me, as well as for the customer.

In May 2017, I understood that I was to bring back the hands-on-healing and to deliver it for free. I was very surprised that I was going to be delivering it again but so deeply happy. I began to tell all those who attended my fitness classes and my personal training clients about it. I delivered this free spiritual healing service in my home. At this time as the majority of my fitness classes were in Hounslow and Southall both areas of high Asian population and my personal training clients lived in these areas too, a lot of the people who came for the spiritual healing were Sikh, Hindu, Muslim and of other religions/spiritual beliefs. Being able to observe God/Spirit/Jesus healing people of all these different religions/spiritual beliefs through me again, gave me so much joy.

In two of the hands-on-healing sessions, a mother in one and a father in another, both who had passed away/transitioned back to the spiritual realm, came through for their adult children. I had also begun to enjoy watching TV shows of mediums bringing messages from Spirit to people on earth. I could see that they were clearly people who had been given a gift from Spirit/God to bring healing. I wanted to know if I had anybody up there championing me. I did some research and I found a medium who had lots of really wonderful testimonials. My appointment was on the 13th July 2017. The first thing he said to me, even before I sat down was "You're a healer aren't you?". I was so surprised and I felt a bit guilty, as if I had kept something away from him, though truly it was great to see what he knew about me straight away. He told me he could feel my healing energy powerfully. My maternal nan came through. I had never met her on earth, as she had transitioned back to the spiritual realm before I was born. The medium said "You drink a lot of green tea, don't you?" I said yes I drink a lot of peppermint tea. He said your nan is laughing, as she is saying it is nothing like the bush mint tea that she used to drink in the Caribbean. Through the medium she told me that the name Power Flower had come from her and the sunflower was the symbol. I later understood that although Power Flower suited my personal training and fitness work, it represented that because of the spiritual healing work that Spirit/God/Jesus was carrying out through me, like a sunflower people would be drawn to His Light. She told me through the medium that she knew I had felt very alone but I had not been alone, as she had been with me every breath. She said she was sorry that I did not have a good mother and for my bad experiences. Hearing her say this made me feel very supported because although it was her own daughter she was speaking about, she only spoke the truth. She said she knew I had the prophetic dreams that stopped. She said I had to clear out really everyone from my life and showed the medium, sweeping everyone out and said "And look at you now." She said I did the right thing and not to feel guilty anymore. She said "Who needs Jesus?", saying that I was too evolved and discerning to be brought into the 'church', as people were trying to do, as they would be teaching that Jesus discriminates due to religion/spiritual belief and sexual orientation, and I know Jesus does not, He is for everyone. She said she liked to read, study and teach herself and I also like to study like her. She spoke of the many of jobs that I had and said she's been with me through all of them. She was laughing as she spoke about this. She spoke about my fitness work and bringing all the different exercises together. She showed the medium the colourful mirror to my side that I had not seen and said that my love of vibrant colours was from her. She also spoke about my love of the ocean and that I was mesmerised by it and this was from her also. She said I was very resourceful, making things out of nothing like her. She said she had come from a background with little but had produced a lot. The medium said she spoke of a child, a sister that I had lost. I did not know at the time who she was referring to but later learnt it was my sister who was miscarried before I was born. She said there were lots of secrets which should have been told. She said I got my emotional strength from her. She said she was waiting for this to happen and that she was my spirit guide. This is most of what she said to me that day.

On the 9th August 2017, I attended a spiritualist church. I did not know what to expect but I wanted to see if it was possible to have another wonderful experience, as I had with my nan on the 13th July 2017. I watched different people receiving messages from their loved ones in the spiritual realm. It was an incredible experience. Due to the number of people in the congregation and the time limit, not everyone can receive a message each service. The medium came to me and said that she had my sister with her. I was amazed as this was the sister who was miscarried before I was born. My sister told the medium what I had been doing that day, that I had been moving furniture around to create space to begin delivering personal training in my home, which was true. She also spoke of my many hairstyles that she had enjoyed with me. She spoke of the reason that I was tired and run down; that I was giving out too much and not giving myself enough. At the time I had a thumb infection which because of the pain and swelling prevented me from being able to drive to deliver my fitness sessions. She said to me through the medium, that my spiritual family were helping me to make changes so that I could balance my time better. My sister said to me they were raising my energy and providing me with some healing. After that day I began to attend this spiritualist church weekly. I love the services there. They have services with hymns and modern services, singing songs such as "I believe in angels" and "I can see clearly now the rain has gone." They are hosted by laypeople, officers of the church and the mediums deliver the main part of the services. The mediums attend the various spiritualist churches in an area, on a rotational basis. Only Love and Light are present. They are for everyone irrespective of religion/spiritual belief and sexual orientation. The messages are to help people grow in the Light and specifically to support people to follow the plan that Spirit/God has for each one of us. The spiritual family members who I receive messages from on a regular basis are my maternal nan who I did not know on the earth plane, my paternal grandma who I did know on the earth plane, my paternal great grandfather who I did not know on the earth plane, my maternal grandfather who I did know on the earth plane, my paternal great grandmother who I did not know on the earth plane and my sister who I did not know on the earth plane. The mediums always first ensure that you have enough evidence, to know that they are really speaking with whom they say they are and then they deliver the messages of Love and Light. It is truly a blessing to have such easy access to clarity from Spirit along our human journey as although we are spiritual beings, we do not have the purview they have, as they live in the spiritual realm. Having been able to see what some religions including the traditional Christian churches teach, which often is to fear engaging with those who have transitioned back to the spiritual realm, I understand their confusion about what Spirit/God sent Jesus to earth to demonstrate. Jesus came to demonstrate the Resurrection of the Dead and show that like He, we would all do the same.

On 5th September 2017, I had a one to one reading with one of the mediums who delivers services at my spiritualist church. One of the messages that my nan gave to me through the medium was that I needed to read more and then I would be able to help many people. She also said to me if I felt the need to speak to someone, the person who was like a brother to me, would be the best person to go to. At the time I did not know who she was referring to. Quite often when you receive messages from Spirit whether they be through a medium or through a hands-on-healing session, the meaning of them unfolds in the future at the perfect Divinely cultivated time. Just over a month later I felt the need to share with my dentist who was also a pastor, a recent development in my spiritual healing. I then realised who my nan was referring to. She knew that I would want to talk about this particular development but also she had directed me there for another reason. Whilst we were talking, he showed me a book: "The Aquarian Gospel of Jesus the Christ by Levi". The moment I saw that it included chapters on the life and works of Jesus in India, Tibet, Persia, Assyria, Greece and Egypt; I knew I wanted to obtain this book as soon as possible. I ordered it when I got home. This was the other reason that my nan sent me to meet with him that day.

I was amazed when I read this book. There were Scriptures which were familiar to me having read the Bible but the differences were significant. What I read in this book resonated in my spirit, with my heart and soul; Divine Love and Truth. The Introduction of this book and the Scriptures contained at the back of this book show this clearly.

Regularly attending my spiritualist church services and reading daily The Aquarian Gospel of Jesus the Christ by Levi, in addition to my own relationship with Spirit/God/Jesus has enabled the light within me to shine strongly. One of the most powerful teachings for me, evidenced in all of these three ways, is that we have lived previous lifetimes before our current lifetime. That we came to earth to learn the lessons, that we still have outstanding from our previous lifetimes. That our challenges in this lifetime are because of what we did wrong in our previous lifetimes. When I first began to understand this, it was an ugly truth to stomach. I realised that in my previous lifetimes:

1) I had been a perpetrator of racial discrimination; hence my experiences of being on the receiving end of racial discrimination.

2) I had neglected my previous children, hence my own experiences of growing up through their eyes, suffering as they did as children.

3) My previous children continued to suffer when they became adults because as I had neglected them when they were children, they did not learn to grow into adults with a sense of self, so learnt to

tolerate abuse, hence my experiences of being on the receiving end of abuse as an adult.

4) I abused my power when I had been given the responsibility of supporting people who were struggling financially and did not show them any compassion, hence my suffering also financially.

As I allowed myself to fully accept these truths, the depth of my remorse deepened. I felt physically uncomfortable for some days and I cried deeply. On one of these days, as I cried a sound came from deep within me. It sounded like a wounded animal. It was a very difficult time but because of the Divine Love and forgiveness of Spirit/God, it eventually passed.

When this passed, I felt a feeling of freedom that I had never felt before. As I understood I had caused all of my afflictions, I was able to let go of all of my thoughts that were about being a victim in this lifetime. I understood that this was all part of serving Spirit/God; to pay our outstanding debts and commit to helping others.

I then understood what forgiveness really was. I realised that all of us on the earth plane are here with outstanding debts; otherwise if we did not have outstanding debts, we would have transitioned back to the spiritual realm as our human lessons would have been learnt. I realised that most of us do not know the pain we have caused others in previous lifetimes, so it is very easy for us to judge one another and choose not to forgive one another. This understanding of forgiveness enabled me to forgive Jane and her husband. I would not be able to have a relationship with either of them but I was able to forgive them. I began to go deep within to fully forgive all of those people who in this lifetime had caused me pain. Forgiving everyone that I needed to, liberated me and created the space for lots of Love and Light to come in; replacing the darkness created by my previous inability to forgive.

In March 2018, I received a message via a medium at my spiritualist church, that Richard was thinking about the things that he had done and said, that he should not have done and said; specifically that he was in a state of repentance. We have been in contact since and are moving forward.

I continue to learn along my journey. Not long ago I finally began to engage with people who were homeless and asking for money. Before I would justify that I should not give them money because they may use it for alcohol/drugs or they may try to attack me. When I began to see them as Spirit/God sees them, they are His children, He loves them and they are hurting, then I was able to connect from my heart.

My main focus now is my thoughts. I pay attention to what I am thinking and my vibration. When I sense a disturbance of peace within my spirit, I know I am not in alignment with Spirit/God.

My spiritual healing work, I know is now what will grow. I have received many messages regarding this work, some of which I have already spoken about. I also received these messages:

"Your voice will be heard on the earth plane."

The violet light, which is of the highest level of healing, was seen over my head.

A blue light indicating clairaudience was seen at my throat.

PEACE, WISDOM & LOVE.

Choosing to go inwards to seek from within, that is, stopping to go into the silence and rituals/practices e.g., walking in nature; art; reading; exercise; prayers; religious clothing; journaling; items such as a cross, crystal, mezuzah; listening to music; chanting; singing; hands-on-healing; dancing; meditation; enjoying pets; messages via mediums; going to churches, temples, mosques, synagogues and other spiritual/religious gatherings:-

Can place one's mind on the Spiritual Plane.

Result = Peace, Wisdom & Love of Spirit/God/Jesus/Higher Power/Higher Energy.

Explore what is best for you, then do all you have identified, as often as you see is necessary, to achieve and maintain:-

Peace, Wisdom & Love in your life.

Scriptures from The Aquarian Gospel of Jesus the Christ by Levi.

THE CUSP OF THE AGES.

In Spirit I was caught away into the realms of Akasha; I stood alone within the circle of the sun.

And there I found the secret spring that opens up the door to Wisdom and an understanding heart.

I entered in and then I knew.

I saw the four and twenty Cherubim and Seraphim that guard the circle of the sun, the mighty ones who were proclaimed by masters long ago 'the four and twenty ancient ones.'

I heard the names of every Cherubim and Seraphim, and learned that every sign in all the Zodiac is ruled by two - a Cherubim and Seraphim.

And then I stood upon the cusp where Ages meet. The Piscean Age had passed; the Aquarian Age had just begun.

I saw the guardian Spirits of the Piscean Age; Ramasa is the Cherubim; Vacabiel is Seraphim.

I saw the guardian Spirits of the Aquarian Age, and Archer is the Cherubim; Sakmaquil is the Seraphim.

These four great spirits of the Triune God stood close together on the cusp, and in the presence of the sacred Three - the God of Might, the God of Wisdom, and the God of Love - the scepter of Domain, of Might, of Wisdom and of Love was there transferred.

I heard the charges of the Triune God; but these I may not now reveal.

I heard the history of the Piscean Age from Piscean Cherubim and Seraphim, and when I took my pen to write Ramasa said:

Not now, my son, not now; but you may write it down for men when men have learned the sacred laws of Brotherhood, of Peace on earth, good-will to every living thing.

And then I heard the Aquarian Cherubim and Seraphim proclaim the Gospel of the coming Age, the age of Wisdom, of the Son of Man.

And when the crown was lifted from the head of Ramasa and placed upon the head of Archer of the Aquarian Age; and when the royal scepter was transferred from Seraphim Vacabiel to Seraphim Sakmaquil there was deep silence in the courts of heaven.

And then the goddess Wisdom spoke, and with her hands outstretched she poured the benedictions of the Holy Breath upon the rulers of Aquarius.

I may not write the words she spoke, but I may tell the Gospel of the coming age that Archer told when he received the crown.

And I may breathe to men the song of praise that Seraphim Sakmaquil sung when she received the royal scepter of the newborn age.

This Gospel I will tell, and I will sing this song in every land, to all the people, tribes and tongues of earth.

THE CHRIST.

Before creation was the Christ walked with the Father God and Mother God in Akasha.

The Christ is son, the only son begotten by Almighty God, the God of Force and God omniscient, God of thought; and Christ is God, the God of Love.

Without the Christ there was no light. Through Christ all life was manifest; and so through him all things were done, and naught was done in forming worlds or peopling worlds without the Christ.

Christ is the Logos of Infinities and through the word alone are Thought and Force made manifest.

The Son is called the Christ, because the Son, the Love, the universal Love, was set apart, ordained to be creator, Lord, preserver and redeemer of all things, of everything that is, or evermore will be.

Through Christ, the protoplast, the earth, the plant, the beast, the man, the angel and the cherubim took up their stations on their planes of life.

Through Christ they are preserved; and if they fall it is the Christ who lifts them up; and if they sell themselves to sin the Christ redeems.

Now Christ, the universal Love, pervades all spaces of infinity, and so there is no end to love.

From the great heart of Love unnumbered spirits were sent forth to demonstrate the height, the depth, the width, the boundlessness of Love.

To every world and star and moon and sun a master spirit of this Love divine was sent; and all were full anointed with the oil of helpfulness, and each became a Christ.

All glorious in his majesty is Christ, who spread the pure white robe of Love o'er all the planes of earth - the Christ of earth, its heaven, its graves.

In course of time the protoplast, the earth, the plant, the beast, the man sold out their birthrights unto sin; but Christ was present to redeem.

Hid in the holiest place in all infinities is locked the scroll that bears the record of the purposes of God, the Triune God, and there we read:

Perfection is the ultimate of life. A seed is perfect in its embryotic life, but it is destined to unfold, to grow.

Into the soil of every plane these seeds, which were the Thoughts of God, were cast - the seeds of protoplast, of earth, of plant, of beast, of man, of angel and of cherubim, and they who sowed the seeds, through Christ, ordained that they should grow, and should return at last, by effort of unnumbered years, to the great granary of thought, and each be a perfection of its kind.

And in the boundless blessedness of Love the man was made the Lord of protoplast, of earth, of plant, of beast; and Christ proclaimed: Man shall have full dominion over everything that is upon these planes of life; and it was so.

And he who gave the lordship unto man declared that he must rule by Love.

But men grew cruel and they lost their power to rule, and protoplast, and earth, and plant and beast became at enmity with man; he lost his heritage; but Christ was present to redeem.

But man had lost his consciousness of right; he could no longer comprehend the boundlessness of Love; he could see naught but self, and things of self; but Christ was there to seek the lost and save.

So that he might be close to man in all the ways of life, that man might comprehend the mighty spirit of the Love, the Christ of earth made manifest to human eyes and ears by taking his abode in some pure person, well prepared by many lives to be a fit abiding place of Love.

Thus Christ made manifest Love's power to save; but men forgot so soon, and so Christ must manifest again, and then again.

And ever since man took his place in form of flesh the Christ has been manifest in flesh at first of every age.

LEVI'S COMMISSION.

And then Visel the holy one stood forth and said:

O Levi, son of man, behold, for you are called to be the message bearer of the coming age - the age of spirit blessedness.

Give heed, O son of man, for men must know the Christ, the Love of God; for Love is sovereign balm for all the wounds of men, the remedy for every ill.

And man must be endowed with Wisdom and with Power and with an Understanding heart.

Behold the Akasha! Behold the Record Galleries of Visel where every thought and word and deed of every living thing is written down.

The needs of men are manifold, and men must know their needs.

Now, Levi, hearken to my words: go forth into these mystic Galleries and read. There you will find a message for the world; for every man; for every living thing.

I breathe upon you now the Holy Breath; you will discriminate, and you will know the lessons that these Record Books of God are keeping now for men of this new age.

This age will be an age of splendor and of light, because it is the home age of the Holy Breath; and Holy Breath will testify anew for Christ, the Logos of eternal Love.

At first of every age this Logos is made manifest in flesh so man can see and know and comprehend a Love that is not narrow, circumscribed.

Twelve times in every revolution of the sun this christed Love of God is made full manifest in flesh upon the planes of earth, and you may read in Akasha the wondrous lessons that these Christs have taught to men; but you shall publish not to men the lessons of the Christs of ancient times.

Now, Levi, message bearer of the Spirit Age, take up your pen and write.

Write full the story of the Christ who built upon the Solid Rock of yonder circle of the sun - the Christ who men have known as Enoch the Initiate.

Write of his works as prophet, priest and seer; write of his life of purity and love, and how he changed his carnal flesh to flesh divine without descending through the gates of death.

And you may write the story of Melchizedec, the Christ who lived when Abram lived, and pointed out to men the way to life through sacrifice; who gave his life a willing sacrifice for men.

And you may write the story of the Prince of Peace, the Christ who came as babe in Bethlehem, and traveled every way of life that man must tread.

He was despised, rejected and abused; was spit upon, was crucified, was buried in a tomb; but he revived and rose a conqueror over death that he might show the possibilities of man.

A thousand times he said to men: 'I came to show the possibilities of man; what I have done all men may do, and what I am all men shall be.'

These stories of the Christ will be enough, for they contain the true philosophy of life, of death and of the resurrection of the dead.

They show the spiral journey of the soul until the man of earth and God are one forevermore.

MAN.

Time never was when man was not.

If life of man at any time began a time would come when it would end.

The thoughts of God cannot be circumscribed. No finite mind can comprehend things infinite.

All finite things are subject unto change. All finite things will cease to be, because there was a time when they were not.

The bodies and the soul of men are finite things, and they will change, yea, from the finite point of view the time will come when they will be no more.

But man himself is not the body, nor the soul; he is a spirit and is part of God.

Creative Fiat gave to man, to spirit man, a soul that he might function on the plane of soul; gave him a body of the flesh, that he might function on the plane of things made manifest.

Why did creative Fiat give to spirit man a soul that he might function on the plane of soul?

Why did creative Fiat give to soul a body of the flesh that it might function on the plane of things that are made manifest?

Hear, now, ye worlds, dominions, powers and thrones!

Hear, now, ye cherubim, ye seraphim, ye angels and ye men!

Hear, now, O protoplast, and earth, and plant and beast!

Hear, now, ye creeping things of earth, ye fish that swim, ye birds that fly!

Hear, now, ye winds that blow, ye thunders and ye lightnings of the sky!

Hear, now, ye spirits of the fire, of water, earth and air!

Hear, now, O everything that is, or was, or evermore will be, for Wisdom speaks from out the highest plane of spirit life:

Man is a thought of God; all thoughts of God are infinite; they are not measured up by time, for things that are concerned with time begin and end.

The thoughts of God are from the everlasting of the past unto the never ending days to come - And so is man, the Spirit-man.

But man, like every other thought of God, was but a seed, a seed that held within itself the potencies of God, just as the seed of any plant of earth holds deep within itself the attributes of every part of that especial plant.

So spirit-man, as seed of God, held deep within himself the attributes of every part of God.

Now, seeds are perfect, yea, as perfect as the source from which they come; but they are not unfolded into life made manifest.

The child in utero is perfect as the mother is.

So man, the seed, must be deep planted in a soil that he might grow, unfold, as does the bud unfold to show the flower.

The human seed that came forth from the heart of God was full ordained to be the lord of plane of soul, and of the plane of things made manifest.

So God, the husbandman of every thing that is, threw forth this human seed into the soil of soul; it grew apace, and man became a living soul; and he became the lord of all the kingdom of the soul.

Hark, now, let every creature hear, The plane of soul is but the ether of the spirit plane vibrating not so fast, and in the slower rhythm of this plane the essences of life are manifest; the perfumes and the odors, the true sensations and the all of love are manifest.

And these soul attributes become a body beautiful.

A multitude of lessons man must learn upon the plane of soul; and here he tarries many ages until his lessons are all learned.

Upon the boundary of the plane of soul the ether began to vibrate slower still, and then the essences took on a garb; the perfumes and the odors and the true sensations and the all of love were clothed in flesh; and man was clothed in flesh.

Perfected man must pass through all the ways of life, and so a carnal nature was full manifest, a nature that sprang forth from fleshly things.

Without a foe a soldier never knows his strength, and thought must be developed by the exercise of strength.

And so this carnal nature soon became a foe that man must fight, that he might be the strength of God made manifest.

Let every living thing stand still and hear!

Man is the lord of all the plane of manifests; of protoplast, of mineral, of plant, of beast; but he has given up his birthright, just to gratify his lower self, his carnal self.

But man will full regain his lost estate, his heritage; but he must do it in a conflict that cannot be told in words.

Yea, he must suffer trials and temptations manifold; but let him know that cherubim and seraphim that rule the stations of the sun, and spirits of the mighty God who rule the solar stars are his protectors and his guides, and they will lead to victory.

Man will be fully saved, redeemed, perfected by the things he suffers on the plane of flesh, and on the plane of soul.

When man has conquered carnal things his garb of flesh will then have served its purpose well and it will fall, will be no more.

Then he will stand untrammeled on the plane of soul where he must full complete his victories.

Unnumbered foes will stand before the man upon the plane of soul; there he must overcome, yea, overcome them every one.

Thus hope will ever be his beacon light; there is no failure for the human soul, for God is leading on and victory is sure.

Man cannot die; the spirit man is one with God, and while God lives man cannot die.

When man has conquered every foe upon the plane of soul the seed will have full opened out, will have unfolded in the Holy Breath.

The garb of soul will then have served its purpose well, and man will need it never more, and it will pass and be no more.

And man will then attain unto the blessedness of perfectness and be at one with God.

CHAPTER 14.

Matheno's lessons. The doctrine of universal law. The power of man to choose and to attain. The benefits of antagonisms. Ancient sacred books. The place of John and Jesus in the world's history.

1. MATHENO and his pupil, John, were talking of the sacred books of olden times, and of the golden precepts they contained, and John exclaimed,
2. These golden precepts are sublime; what need have we of other sacred books?
3. Matheno said, The Spirits of the Holy One cause every thing to come and go in proper time.
4. The sun has his own time to set, the moon to rise, to wax and wane, the stars to come and go, the rain to fall, the winds to blow;
5. The seed times and the harvest times to come; man to be born and man to die.
6. These mighty Spirits cause the nations to be born; they rock them in their cradles, nurture them to greatest power, and when their tasks are done they wrap them in their winding sheets and lay them in their tombs.
7. Events are many in a nation's life, and in the life of man, that are not pleasant for the time; but in the end the truth appears: whatever comes is for the best.
8. Man was created for a noble part; but he could not be made a free man filled with wisdom, truth and might.
9. If he were hedged about, confined in straits from which he could not pass, then he would be a toy, a mere machine.
10. Creative spirits gave to man a will; and so he

has the power to choose.
11. He may attain the greatest heights, or sink to deepest depths; for what he wills to gain he has the power to gain.
12. If he desires strength he has the power to gain that strength; but he must overcome resistances to reach the goal; no strength is ever gained in idleness.
13. So, in the whirl of many-sided conflicts man is placed where he must strive to extricate himself.
14. In every conflict man gains strength; with every conquest he attains to greater heights. With every day he finds new duties and new cares.
15. Man is not carried over dangerous pits, nor helped to overcome his foes. He is himself his army, and his sword and shield; and he is captain of his hosts.
16. The Holy Ones just light his way. Man never has been left without a beacon light to guide.
17. And he has ever had a lighted lamp in hand that he may see the dangerous rocks, the turbid streams and treacherous pits.
18. And so the Holy Ones have judged; when men have needed added light a master soul has come to earth to give the light.
19. Before the Vedic days the world had many sacred books to light the way; and when man needed greater light the Vedas, the Avesta and the books of Tao Great appeared to show the way to greater heights.

20. And in the proper place the Hebrew Bible, with its Law, its Prophets and its Psalms, appeared for man's enlightenment.
21. But years have passed and men have need of greater light.
22. And now the Day Star from on high begins to shine; and Jesus is the flesh-made messenger to show that light to men.
23. And you, my pupil, you have been ordained to harbinger the coming day.
24. But you must keep that purity of heart you now possess; and you must light your lamp directly from the coals that burn upon the altar of the Holy Ones.
25. And then your lamp will be transmuted to a boundless flame, and you will be a living torch whose light will shine wherever man abides.
26. But in the ages yet to come, man will attain to greater heights, and lights still more intense will come.
27. And then, at last, a mighty master soul will come to earth to light the way up to the throne of perfect man.

CHAPTER 30.

Jesus receives news of the death of his father. He writes a letter to his mother. The letter. He sends it on its way by a merchant.

1. ONE day as Jesus stood beside the Ganges busy with his work, a caravan, returning from the West, drew near.
2. And one, approaching Jesus, said, We come to you just from your native land and bring unwelcome news.
3. Your father is no more on earth; your mother grieves; and none can comfort her. She wonders whether you are still alive or not; she longs to see you once again.
4. And Jesus bowed his head in silent thought; and then he wrote. Of what he wrote this is the sum:
5. My mother, noblest of womankind; A man just from my native land has brought me word that father is no more in flesh, and that you grieve, and are disconsolate.
6. My mother, all is well; is well for father and is well for you.
7. His work in this earth-round is done, and it is nobly done.
8. In all the walks of life men cannot charge him with deceit, dishonesty, nor wrong intent.
9. Here in this round he finished many heavy tasks, and he has gone from hence prepared to solve the problems of the round of soul.
10. Our Father-God is with him there, as he was with him here; and there his angel guards his footsteps lest he goes astray.
11. Why should you weep? Tears cannot conquer grief. There is no power in grief to mend a broken

heart.

12. The plane of grief is idleness; the busy soul can never grieve; it has no time for grief.

13. When grief comes trooping through the heart, just lose yourself; plunge deep into the ministry of love, and grief is not.

14. Yours is a ministry of love, and all the world is calling out for love.

15. Then let the past go with the past; rise from the cares of carnal things and give your life for those who live.

16. And if you lose your life in serving life you will be sure to find in it the morning sun, the evening dews, in song of bird, in flowers, and in the stars of night.

17. In just a little while your problems of this earth-round will be solved; and when your sums are all worked out it will be pleasure unalloyed for you to enter wider fields of usefulness, to solve the greater problems of the soul.

18. Strive, then, to be content, and I will come to you some day and bring you richer gifts than gold or precious stones.

19. I'm sure that John will care for you, supplying all your needs; and I am with you all the way, Jehoshua.

20. And by the hand of one, a merchant, going to Jerusalem, he sent this letter on its way.

CHAPTER 40.

Jesus teaches the magians. Explains the Silence and how to enter it. Kaspar extols the wisdom of Jesus. Jesus teaches in the groves of Cyrus.

1. NOW, in the early morning Jesus came again to teach and heal. A light not comprehended shown about, as though some mighty spirit overshadowed him.
2. A magus noted this and asked him privately to tell from whence his wisdom came, and what the meaning of the light.
3. And Jesus said, There is a Silence where the soul may meet its God, and there the fount of wisdom is, and all who enter are immersed in light, and filled with wisdom, love and power.
4. The magus said, Tell me about this Silence and this light, that I may go and there abide.
5. And Jesus said, The Silence is not circumscribed; is not a place closed in with wall, or rocky steeps, nor guarded by the sword of man.
6. Men carry with them all the time the secret place where they may meet their God.
7. It matters not where men abide, on mountain top, in deepest vale, in marts of trade, or in the quiet home; they may at once, at any time, fling wide the door, and find the Silence, find the house of God; it is within the soul.
8. One may not be so much disturbed by noise of

business, and the words and thoughts of men if he goes all alone into the valley or the mountain pass.
9. And when life's heavy load is pressing hard, it is far better to go out and seek a quiet place to pray and meditate.
10. The Silence is the kingdom of the soul which is not seen by human eyes.
11. When in the Silence, phantom forms may flit before the mind; but they are all subservient to the will; the master soul may speak and they are gone.
12. If you would find this Silence of the soul you must yourself prepare the way. None but the pure in heart may enter here.
13. And you must lay aside all tenseness of the mind, all business cares, all fears, all doubts and troubled thoughts.
14. Your human will must be absorbed by the divine; then you will come into a consciousness of holiness.
15. You are within the Holy Place, and you will see upon a living shrine the candle of the Lord aflame.
16. And when you see it burning there, look deep into the temple of your brain, and you will see it all aglow.
17. In every part, from head to foot, are candles all in place, just waiting to be lighted by the flaming torch of love.
18. And when you see the candles all aflame, just look, and you will see, with eyes of soul, the waters of the fount of wisdom rushing on; and you may

drink, and there abide.

19. And then the curtains part, and you are in the Holiest of All, where rests the Ark of God, whose covering is the Mercy Seat.

20. Fear not to lift the sacred board; the Tables of the Law are in the Ark concealed.

21. Take them and read them well; for they contain all precepts and commands that men will ever need.

22. And in the Ark, the magic wand of prophecy lies waiting for your hand; it is the key to all the hidden meanings of the present, future, past.

23. And then, behold, the manna there, the hidden bread of life; and he who eats shall never die.

24. The cherubim have guarded well for every soul this treasure box, and whosoever will may enter in and find his own.

25. Now Kaspar heard the Hebrew master speak and he exclaimed, Behold, the wisdom of the gods has come to men!

26. And Jesus went his way, and in the sacred groves of Cyrus, where the multitudes were met, he taught and healed the sick.

CHAPTER 94.

The Sermon on the Mount. Jesus reveals to the twelve the secret of prayer. The model prayer. The law of forgiveness. The holy fast. The evil of deceit. Almsgiving.

1. NEXT morning e'er the sun had risen Jesus and the twelve went to a mountain near the sea to pray; and Jesus taught the twelve disciples how to pray. He said,
2. Prayer is the deep communion of the soul with God;
3. So when you pray do not deceive yourselves as do the hypocrites who love to stand upon the streets and in the synagogues and pour out many words to please the ears of men.
4. And they adorn themselves with pious airs that they may have the praise of men. They seek the praise of men and their reward is sure.
5. But when you pray, go to the closet of your soul; close all the doors, and in the holy silence, pray.
6. You need not speak a multitude of words, nor yet repeat the words again and then again, as heathen do. Just say,
7. Our Father-God who art in heaven; holy is thy name. Thy kingdom come; thy will be done on earth as it is done in heaven.
8. Give us this day our needed bread;
9. Help us forget the debts that other people owe to us, that all our debts may be discharged.
10. And shield us from the tempter's snares that are too great for us to bear;
11. And when they come give us the strength to overcome.
12. If you would be discharged from all the debts you owe to God and man, the debts you have

incurred by wilfully transgressing law,
13. You must pass by the debts of every man; for as you deal with other men your God will deal with you.
14. And when you fast you may not advertise the deed.
15. When fast the hypocrites they paint their faces, look demure, assume a pious pose, that they may seem to men to fast.
16. A fast is deed of soul, and like a prayer, it is a function of the silence of the soul.
17. God never passes by unnoticed any prayer, or fast. He walks within the silence, and his benedictions rest on every effort of the soul.
18. Deception is hypocrisy, and you shall not assume to be what you are not.
19. You may not clothe yourselves in special garb to advertise your piety, nor yet assume the tone of voice that men conceive to be a holy voice.
20. And when you give to aid the needy ones, blow not a trumpet in the street, nor synagogue to advertise your gift.
21. He who does alms for praise of men has his reward from men; but God regardeth not.
22. In giving alms do not let the right hand know the secret of the left.

CHAPTER 114.

A great storm on the sea destroys many lives. Jesus makes an appeal for aid, and the people give with a generous hand. In answer to a lawyer's question, Jesus gives the philosophy of disasters.

1. AS Jesus taught, a man stood forth and said, Rabboni, may I speak?
2. And Jesus said, Say on. And then the man spoke out and said,
3. A storm upon the sea last night wrecked many fishing boats, and scores of men went down to death, and, lo, their wives and children are in need;
4. What can be done to help them in their sore distress?
5. And Jesus said, A worthy plea. You men of Galilee, take heed. We may not bring again to live these men, but we can succor those who looked to them for daily bread.
6. You stewards of the wealth of God, an opportunity has come; unlock your vaults; bring forth your hoarded gold; bestow it with a lavish hand.
7. This wealth was laid aside for just such times as these; when it was needed not, lo, it was yours to guard;
8. But now it is not yours, for it belongs to those who are in want, and if you give it not you simply bring upon your heads the wrath of God.

9. It is not charity to give to those who need; it is but honesty; it is but giving men their own.
10. Then Jesus turned to Judas, one of the twelve, who was the treasurer of the band, and said,
11. Bring forth our treasure box; the money is not ours now; turn every farthing to the help of those in such distress.
12. Now, Judas did not wish to give the money all to those in want, and so he talked with Peter, James and John.
13. He said, Lo, I will save a certain part and give the rest; that surely is enough for us, for we are strangers to the ones in want; we do not even know their names.
14. But Peter said, Why, Judas, man, how do you dare to think to trifle with the strength of right.
15. The Lord has spoken true; this wealth does not belong to us in face of this distress, and to refuse to give it is to steal.
16. You need not fear; we will not come to want.
17. Then Judas opened up the treasure box and gave the money all.
18. And there was gold and silver, food, and raiment in abundance for the needs of the bereaved.
19. A lawyer said, Rabboni, if God rules the worlds and all that in them is, did he not bring about this storm? did he not slay these men?
20. Has he not brought this sore distress upon these people here? and was it done to punish them for

crimes?

21. And we remember well when once a band of earnest Jews from Galilee were in Jerusalem, and at a feast and were, for fancied crimes against the Roman law,

22. Cut down within the very temple court by Pontius Pilate; and their blood became their sacrifice.

23. Did God bring on this slaughter all because these men were doubly vile?

24. And then we bring to mind that once a tower called Siloam, graced the defences of Jerusalem, and, seemingly, without a cause it tottered and it fell to earth and eighteen men were killed.

25. Were these men vile? and were they slain as punishment for some great crime?

26. And Jesus said, We cannot look upon a single span of life and judge of anything.

27. There is a law that men must recognize: Result depends on cause.

28. Men are not motes to float about within the air of one short life, and then be lost in nothingness.

29. They are undying parts of the eternal whole that come and go, lo, many times into the air of earth and of the great beyond, just to unfold the God-like self.

30. A cause may be a part of one brief life; results may not be noted till another life.

31. The cause of your results cannot be found within my life, nor can the cause of my results be found in yours.

32. I cannot reap except I sow and I must reap whate'er I sow,

33. The law of all eternities is known to master minds:

34. Whatever men do unto other men the judge and executioner will do to them.

35. We do not note the execution of this law among the sons of men.

36. We note the weak dishonored, trampled on and slain by those men call the strong.

37. We note that men with wood-like heads are seated in the chairs of state;

38. Are kings and judges, senators and priests, while men with giant intellects are scavengers about the streets.

39. We note that women with a moiety of common sense, and not a whit of any other kind, are painted up and dressed as queens,

40. Becoming ladies of the courts of puppet kings, because they have the form of something beautiful; while God's own daughters are their slaves, or serve as common laborers in the field.

41. The sense of justice cries aloud: This is a travesty on right.

42. So when men see no further than one little span of life it is no wonder that they say, There is no God, or if there is a God he is a tyrant and should die.

43. If you would judge aright of human life, you

must arise and stand upon the crest of time and note the thoughts and deeds of men as they have come up through the ages past;

44. For we must know that man is not a creature made of clay to turn again to clay and disappear.

45. He is a part of the eternal whole. There never was a time when he was not; a time will never come when he will not exist.

46. And now we look; the men who now are slaves were tyrants once; the men who now are tyrants have been slaves.

47. The men who suffer now, once stood aloft and shouted with a fiend's delight while others suffered at their hands.

48. And men are sick, and halt, and lame, and blind because they once transgressed the laws of perfect life, and every law of God must be fulfilled.

49. Man may escape the punishment that seems but due for his mis-doings in this life; but every deed and word and thought has its own metes and bounds,

50. Its cause, and has its own results, and if a wrong be done, the doer of the wrong must make it right.

51. And when the wrongs have all been righted then will man arise and be at one with God.

CHAPTER 138.

The Christines in Jerusalem. They meet a man blind from birth. Jesus teaches a lesson on the cause of disease and disasters. He heals the blind man.

1. THE Lord with Peter, James and John were in Jerusalem; it was the Sabbath day.
2. And as they walked along the way they saw a man who could not see; he had been blind from birth.
3. And Peter said, Lord, if disease and imperfections all are caused by sin, who was the sinner in this case? the parents or the man himself?
4. And Jesus said, Afflictions all are partial payments on a debt, or debts, that have been made.
5. There is a law of recompense that never fails, and it is summarized in that true rule of life:
6. Whatsoever man shall do to any other man some other man will do to him.
7. In this we find the meaning of the Jewish law, expressed concisely in the words, Tooth for a tooth; life for a life.
8. He who shall injure any one in thought, or word, or deed, is judged a debtor to the law, and some one else shall, likewise, injure him in thought, or word or deed.
9. And he who sheds the blood of any man will come upon the time when his blood shall be shed by man.

10. Affliction is a prison cell in which a man must stay until he pays his debts unless a master sets him free that he may have a better chance to pay his debts.
11. Affliction is a certain sign that one has debts to pay.
12. Behold this man! Once in another life he was a cruel man, and in a cruel way destroyed the eyes of one, a fellow man.
13. The parents of this man once turned their faces on a blind and helpless man, and drove him from their door.
14. Then Peter asked, Do we pay off the debts of other men when by the Word we heal them, drive the unclean spirits out, or rescue them from any form of sore distress?
15. And Jesus said, We cannot pay the debts of any man, but by the Word we may release a man from his afflictions and distress,
16. And make him free, that he may pay the debts he owes, by giving up his life in willing sacrifice for men, or other living things.
17. Behold, we may make free this man that he may better serve the race and pay his debts.
18. Then Jesus called the man and said, Would you be free? would you receive your sight?
19. The man replied, All that I have would I most freely give if I could see.
20. And Jesus took saliva and a bit of clay and made a salve, and put it on the blind man's eyes.

21. He spoke the Word and then he said, Go to Siloam and wash, and as you wash say, *Jahhevahe*. This do for seven times and you shall see.

22. The man was led unto Siloam; he washed his eyes and spoke the word, and instantly his eyes were opened and he saw.

23. The people who had seen the man for many years sit by the way and beg, were much surprised to see him see.

24. They said, Is not this man the Job that was born blind, who sat beside the way and begged?

25. He heard them talk among themselves; he said, Yes, I am he.

26. The people asked, How were you healed? who opened up your eyes?

27. He said, A man whom men call Jesus, made a salve of clay and put it on my eyes, and bade me say a word and wash in Siloam seven times; I did as he commanded me, and now I see.

28. A certain scribe was passing, and he saw the man and heard him say that Jesus, by the Word, had opened up his eyes.

29. He therefore took the man up to the synagogue, and told the story to the priests, who asked the man about the miracle.

30. The man replied, I never saw the light until today, for I was blind from birth.

31. This morning as I sat beside Siloam, a man I never knew put on my eyes a salve that people say he made of clay; he bade me say a word and bathe my eyes in water seven times; I did as he commanded and I saw.

32. A lawyer asked the man, Who was it opened up your eyes?

33. The man replied, Some people say, His name is Jesus and that he came from Galilee; but others say, He is the son of God.

34. A Pharisee came up and said, This is the Sabbath day; a man who does a work like this, regarding not the Sabbath day, is not from God.

35. Some of the priests were much amazed and said, A wicked man could never do a miracle like this; he must possess the power of God. And so they strove among themselves.

36. They asked the man, What do you think about this man from Galilee?

37. He said, He is a prophet sent from God.

38. Now, many of the Jews did not believe the man was blind from birth; they said, There is no power to open up the eyes of one born blind.

39. And then they brought the parents of the man before the Pharisees that they might testify.

40. They said, This is our son who was born blind; we do not know how he received his sight; he is of age and he can tell; ask him.

41. They were afraid to say what they believed, that Jesus is the Christ who came to manifest the power of God, lest they offend the priests and be cast from the synagogue.

42. Again the rulers said, This Jesus is a wicked

man. The man who had been healed stood forth again and said,

43. This Jesus may be sinner or be saint, I do not know; but this one thing I know; I once was blind, but now I see.

44. And then the scribes and Pharisees reviled the man and said, You are a follower of this man from Galilee. We follow Moses, but this man, we know him not, and know not whence he is.

45. The man replied, It is a marvel that you know not whence he is, and yet he opened up my eyes.

46. You know that nothing but the power of God can do such things.

47. God hears not sinners pray, and you must know that he is not a wicked man who can employ the power of God.

48. The Pharisees replied, You wretch! you were begotten and were born in sin, and now you try to teach the law to us. And then they cast him from the synagogue.

CHAPTER 142.

The path of discipleship, its difficulties. The cross and its meaning. The danger of wealth. The young man who loved wealth more than he loved Christ. Parable of the rich man and Lazarus.

1. NOW, Jesus and the twelve went to another town, and as they entered it they said, Peace be to

all; good will to all.
2. A multitude of people followed and the master said to them, Behold, for you are followers for selfish gain.
3. If you would follow me in love, and be disciples of the Holy Breath, and gain at last the crown of life, you must leave all there is of carnal life behind.
4. Be not deceived; stay, men, and count the cost.
5. If one would build a tower, or a home, he first sits down and counts the cost to be assured that he has gold enough to finish it.
6. For well he knows that if he makes a failure of his enterprise he may lose all his wealth, and be the butt of ridicule.
7. And if a king desires to take the kingdom of another king, he calls his trusted men and they consider well their strength; he will not measure arms with one of matchless power.
8. Count well the cost before you start to follow me; it means the giving up of life, and all you have.
9. If you love father, mother, wife, or child, more than you love the Christ, you cannot follow me.
10. If you love wealth or honor more than you love the Christ, you cannot follow me.
11. The paths of carnal life do not run up the mountain side towards the top; they run around the mount of life, and if you go straight to the upper gate of consciousness you cross the paths of carnal life; tread in them not.
12. And this is how men bear the cross; no man can

bear another's cross.

13. Take up your cross and follow me through Christ into the path of true discipleship; this is the path that leads to life.

14. This way of life is called the pearl of greatest price, and he who finds it must put all he has beneath his feet.

15. Behold, a man found in a certain field the croppings of a wondrous mine of gold, and he went forth and sold his home and all he had and bought the field; then he rejoiced in wealth.

16. Now, there were present, scribes and Pharisees of wealth who loved their money, and their bonds and lands, and they laughed loud to scorn what Jesus said.

17. Then Jesus spoke to them and said, You are the men who justify yourselves in sight of men; God knows your wickedness of heart;

18. And you must know, O men, that whatsoever is revered and is exalted by the carnal mind, is an abomination in the sight of God.

19. And Jesus went his way, and as he went a young man ran and knelt down at his feet and said, Good master, tell me what to do that I may have eternal life.

20. And Jesus said, Why do you call me good? No one is truly good but God himself.

21. And God has said, If you would enter into life, keep the Commandments of the law.

22. The young man asked, To which commands did

he refer?
23. And Jesus said, You shall not kill; you shall not steal; you shall not do adulterous things; you shall not falsely testify;
24. And you shall love your God with all your heart, and you shall love your neighbor as yourself.
25. The man replied, These things I have observed from youth; what lack I yet?
26. And Jesus said, One thing you lack; your heart is fixed on things of earth; you are not free.
27. Go forth and sell all that you have, and give your money to the poor, and come and follow me, and you shall have eternal life.
28. The man was grieved at what the master said; for he was rich; he hid his face and went in sorrow on his way.
29. And Jesus looked upon the sorrowing man and said, It is so hard for men with hoarded wealth to enter through the door into the kingdom of the soul.
30. And his disciples were amazed at what he said.
31. He answered them and said, I tell you, men, that they who trust in riches cannot trust in God and cannot come into the kingdom of the soul;
32. Yea, it is easier for a camel to go through a needle's eye than for a man with hoarded wealth to find the way of life. And his disciples said, Who then can find the way? Who can be saved?
33. And Jesus said, The rich may give his gold away; the high may kiss the dust, and God will

save.
34. Then Jesus spoke this parable to them:
35. A rich man lived in splendid state; he wore the finest garments men could make; his boards were loaded with the costliest viands of the land.
36. A beggar, blind and lame, whose name was Lazarus, was wont to sit beside the waste gate of this home that he might share with dogs the refuse from the rich man's boards.
37. It came to pass that Lazarus died, and angels carried him away unto the bosom of our father Abraham.
38. The rich man also died, and he was buried in a costly tomb; but in the purifying fires he opened up his eyes dissatisfied.
39. He looked and saw the beggar resting peacefully in the bosom of his father Abraham, and in the bitterness of his soul he cried,
40. My father Abraham, look down in mercy on your son; I am tormented in these flames.
41. Send Lazarus, I beseech, that he may give me just a sup of water to cool my parched tongue.
42. But Abraham replied, My son, in mortal life, you had the best things of the earth and Lazarus had the worst, and you would not give him a cup of water there, but drove him from your door.
43. The law must be fulfilled, and Lazarus now is comforted, and you are paying what you owe.
44. Besides, there is a great gulf fixed between your zone and us, and if I would I could not send

Lazarus to you, and you cannot come up to us till you have paid your debts.

45. Again the man in anguish said, O father Abraham, I pray, send Lazarus back to earth, and to my father's house, that he may tell my brothers who are yet in life, for I have five of them, about the horrors of this place, lest they come down to me and not to you.

46. And Abraham replied, They have the words of Moses and the seers, let them hear them.

47. The man replied, They will not hearken to the written word; but if a man would go up from the grave they might believe.

48. But Abraham replied, If they hear not the words of Moses and the seers they would not be persuaded even though one from the dead stood in their midst.

49. And Peter said, Lord, we have left our all to follow you; and what is our reward?

50. And Jesus said, Most verily I say to you, that you who have left all to follow me shall come into a newness of a life hid deep with Christ in God.

51. And you shall sit with me upon the throne of power, and judge with me the tribes of Israel.

52. And he who conquers carnal self, and follows me through Christ shall have a hundred fold of that which is the wealth of life on earth, and in the world to come, eternal life.

CHAPTER 176.

Jesus appears, fully materialized, to the eastern sages in the palace of Prince Ravanna in India. To the magian priests in Persia. The three wise men speak in praise of the personality of the Nazarene.

1. RAVANNA, prince of India, gave a feast. His palace in Orissa was the place where men of thought from all the farther East were wont to meet.
2. Ravanna was the prince with whom child Jesus went to India many years ago.
3. The feast was made in honor of the wise men of the East.
4. Among the guests were Meng-ste, Vidyapati and Lamaas.
5. The wise men sat about the table talking of the needs of India and the world.
6. The door unto the banquet hall was in the east; a vacant chair was at the table to the east.
7. And as the wise men talked a stranger entered, unannounced; and raising up his hands in benediction said, All hail!
8. A halo rested on his head, and light, unlike the light of sun, filled all the room.
9. The wise men rose and bowed their heads and said, All hail!
10. And Jesus sat down in the vacant chair; and then the wise men knew it was the Hebrew prophet

who had come.

11. And Jesus said, Behold, for I am risen from the dead. Look at my hands, my feet, my side.

12. The Roman soldiers pierced my hands and feet with nails; and then one pierced my heart.

13. They put me in a tomb, and then I wrestled with the conqueror of men. I conquered death, I stamped upon him and arose;

14. Brought immortality to light and painted on the walls of time a rainbow for the sons of men; and what I did all men shall do.

15. This gospel of the resurrection of the dead is not confined to Jew and Greek; it is the heritage of every man of every time and clime; and I am here a demonstration of the power of man.

16. Then he arose and pressed the hand of every man and of the royal host, and said,

17. Behold, I am not myth made of the fleeting winds, for I am flesh and bone and brawn; but I can cross the borderland at will.

18. And then they talked together there a long, long time. Then Jesus said,

19. I go my way, but you shall go to all the world and preach the gospel of the omnipotence of man, the power of truth, the resurrection of the dead;

20. He who believes this gospel of the son of man shall never die; the dead shall live again.

21. Then Jesus disappeared, but he had sown the seed. The words of life were spoken in Orissa, and all of India heard.

22. The magian priests were in the silence in Persepolis, and Kaspar, and the magian masters who were first to greet the child of promise in the shepherd's home in Bethlehem, were with the priests.
23. And Jesus came and sat with them; a crown of light was on his head.
24. And when the silence ended Kaspar said, A master from the royal council of the Silent Brotherhood is here; let us give praise.
25. And all the priests and masters stood and said, All hail! What message from the royal council do you bring?
26. And Jesus said, My brothers of the Silent Brotherhood, peace, peace on earth; good will to men!
27. The problem of the ages has been solved; a son of man has risen from the dead; has shown that human flesh can be transmuted into flesh divine.
28. Before the eyes of men this flesh in which I come to you was changed with speed of light from human flesh. And so I am the message that I bring to you.
29. To you I come, the first of all the race to be transmuted to the image of the AM.
30. What I have done, all men will do; and what I am, all men will be.
31. But Jesus said no more. In one short breath he told the story of his mission to the sons of men, and then he disappeared.

32. The magi said, Some time ago we read this promise, now fulfilled, upon the dial plate of heaven.
33. And then we saw this man who has just demonstrated unto us the power of man to rise from carnal flesh and blood to flesh of God, a babe in Bethlehem.
34. And after many years he came and sat with us in these same groves;
35. He told the story of his human life, of trials, sore temptations, buffetings and woes.
36. He pressed along the thorny way of life till he had risen and o'er-thrown the strongest foes of God and man; and he is now the only master of the human race whose flesh has been transmuted into flesh divine.
37. He is the God-man of today; but every one of earth shall overcome and be like him, a son of God.

CHAPTER 178.

Jesus appears, fully materialized, before Apollo and the Silent Brotherhood in Greece. Appears to Claudas and Juliet on the Tiber near Rome. Appears to the priests in the Egyptian temple at Heliopolis.

1. APOLLO, with the Silent Brotherhood of Greece, was sitting in a Delphian grove. The Oracle had spoken loud and long.
2. The priests were in the sanctuary and as they

looked the Oracle became a blaze of light; it seemed to be on fire, and all consumed.

3. The priests were filled with fear. They said, A great disaster is to come; our gods are mad; they have destroyed our Oracle.

4. But when the flames had spent themselves, a man stood on the orac pedestal and said,

5. God speaks to man, not by an oracle of wood and gold, but by the voice of man.

6. The gods have spoken to the Greeks, and kindred tongues, through images made by man; but God, the One, now speaks to man through Christ the only son, who was, and is and evermore will be.

7. This Oracle shall fail; the Living Oracle of God, the One, will never fail.

8. Apollo knew the man who spoke; he knew it was the Nazarene who once had taught the wise men in the Acropolis and had rebuked the idol worshippers upon the Athen's beach;

9. And in a moment Jesus stood before Apollo and the Silent Brotherhood, and said,

10. Behold, for I have risen from the dead with gifts for men. I bring to you the title of your vast estate.

11. All power in heaven and earth is mine; to you I give all power in heaven and earth.

12. Go forth and teach the nations of the earth the gospel of the resurrection of the dead and of eternal life through Christ, the love of God made manifest to men.

13. And then he clasped Apollo's hand and said,

My human flesh was changed to higher form by love divine and I can manifest in flesh, or in the higher planes of life, at will.
14. What I can do all men can do. Go preach the gospel of the omnipotence of man.
15. Then Jesus disappeared; but Greece and Crete and all the nations heard.
16. Claudas and Juliet, his wife, lived on the Palatine in Rome and they were servants of Tiberius; but they had been in Galilee;
17. Had walked with Jesus by the sea, had heard his words and seen his power; and they believed that he was Christ made manifest.
18. Now Claudas and his wife were on the Tiber in a little boat; a storm swept from the sea, the boat was wrecked and Claudas and his wife were sinking down to death.
19. And Jesus came and took them by the hands and said, Claudas and Juliet, arise and walk with me upon the waves.
20. And they arose and walked with him upon the waves.
21. A thousand people saw the three walk on the waves, and saw them reach the land, and they were all amazed.
22. And Jesus said, You men of Rome, I am the resurrection and the life. They that are dead shall live, and many that shall live will never die.
23. By mouth of gods and demi-gods God spoke unto your fathers long ago; but now he speaks to

you through perfect man.

24. He sent his son, the Christ, in human flesh, to save the world, and as I lifted from the watery grave and saved these servants of Tiberius,

25. So Christ will lift the sons and daughters of the human race, yea, every one of them, from darkness and from graves of carnal things, to light and everlasting life.

26. I am the manifest of love raised from the dead; Behold my hands, my feet, my side which carnal men have pierced.

27. Claudas and Juliet, whom I have saved from death, are my ambassadors to Rome.

28. And they will point the way and preach the gospel of the Holy Breath and of the resurrection of the dead.

29. And that was all he said, but Rome and all of Italy heard.

30. The priests of Heliopolis were in their temple met to celebrate the resurrection of their brother Nazarite; they knew that he had risen from the dead.

31. The Nazarite appeared and stood upon a sacred pedestal on which no man had ever stood.

32. This was an honor that had been reserved for him who first would demonstrate the resurrection of the dead.

33. And Jesus was the first of all the human race to demonstrate the resurrection of the dead.

34. When Jesus stood upon the sacred pedestal the

masters stood and said, All hail! The great bells of the temple rang and all the temple was ablaze with light.

35. And Jesus said, All honor to the masters of this Temple of the Sun.

36. In flesh of man there is the essence of the resurrection of the dead. This essence, quickened by the Holy Breath, will raise the substance of the body to a higher tone,

37. And make it like the substance of the bodies of the planes above, which human eyes cannot behold.

38. There is a holy ministry in death. The essence of the body cannot be quickened by the Holy Breath until the fixed is solved; the body must disintegrate, and this is death.

39. And then upon these pliant substances God breathes, just as he breathed upon the chaos of the deep when worlds were formed,

40. And life springs forth from death; the carnal form is changed to form divine.

41. The will of man makes possible the action of the Holy Breath. When will of man and will of God are one, the resurrection is a fact.

42. In this we have the chemistry of mortal life, the ministry of death, the mystery of deific life.

43. My human life was wholly given to bring my will to tune with the deific will; when this was done my earth-tasks all were done.

44. And you, my brothers, know full well the foes I

had to meet; you know about my victories in Gethsemane; my trials in the courts of men; my death upon the cross.

45. You know that all my life was one great drama for the sons of men; a pattern for the sons of men. I lived to show the possibilities of man.

46. What I have done all men can do, and what I am all men shall be.

47. The masters looked; the form upon the sacred pedestal had gone, but every temple priest, and every living creature said, Praise God.

Hands-on-Healing Testimonials.

1. I took a 40 minute session and I could feel all what she was doing to me but I was drifting off into a sleep. I could hear myself snoring. After the session, I heard her say quietly; "when you're ready, slowly open your eyes". I opened my eyes and was lying there for a few minutes. Then I sat up. I said to her "say something to me". I put my finger in my left ear. She explained that she does not usually say much after a session, so people can continue to relax in the peace that the healing session brings, however if I felt like talking, that I should do so. And even though she said this so quietly, I heard it. And I told her something she did not know. That I was partially deaf in my right ear and I would either turn my head to hear with my left ear and lip read or wear hearing aids. It was like having water in your ear that would not pop when you yawned and on top of that a loud throbbing sensation. I said to her, "you said that so quietly but I heard it." She was astonished. I went to the bathroom and cried. Then she said "how do you feel?" I said "fine." She really didn't know that I believed in Indigo Swan and that I believed because this was her time, that is why she changed and it was for the better; to help herself and others. I was tested at the Imperial College Healthcare NHS Trust, Charing Cross Hospital, Ear Nose and Throat Specialist Team [ENT] 4 years ago, on 27th May 2010 and they confirmed that I had a hearing loss in my right ear of 60 decibels. This level of hearing loss is classified as Moderately Severe. "She is really suffering from the lack of her hearing..." Consultant ENT Surgeon, in letter to Doctor. They fitted me with 2 hearing aids, a strong one for my right ear and a weak one for my left ear. I have not worn the hearing aids since the session and at work they have noticed I haven't been shouting. Where I work, they play music, so I would be shouting to hear myself above the music. I believe in Jesus and Jesus is within her. Things have changed for me and I have been telling her about them. In the last week, things have been happening to me at work, things are going great and my team members at work have been asking me questions. It is very strange but I walked in on 2 guys talking about; 'is there a God?' I answered to the best of my ability but I told them the next day to go on Indigo Swan's website. Also good news from my hospital results for another medical matter, I got the all clear. This is so good. I was re-tested at InHealth, Fulham Health Clinic [NHS Contract Services], Audiology Health Clinic on 26th June 2014 and they confirmed that [following my Indigo Swan Hands on Healing session on 23rd January 2014], I now have a hearing loss in my right ear of 35 decibels. This level of hearing loss is classified as Mild. I will be fitted on 17th July 2014 with 1 hearing aid for my right ear, to reflect my increased hearing ability.

2. I arrived at Anthea's lovely home looking forward to the healing session. I was greeted by the lovely Anthea complete with yellow flower in her hair. After a short natter (as you do), I was asked to sit in a comfortable chair, relax and close my eyes. Anthea placed her hand on my head for five minutes, during which time I saw images of arches. After the five minutes, I opened my eyes feeling very relaxed and ready to take on the world. My healing session coincided with the anniversary of the death of my father, who was one of the loveliest men in the world. Following the spiritual healing, I went to the crematorium and realised that the images of the arches which came to me were like the arches at the crematorium where my dad's ashes were placed. This indicates to me that he is still with me and wanted to reinforce this fact. How lucky was I. Thank you Anthea you are a gem - very spiritual indeed.

3. I had gout for 2 months. Doctors sent me to hospital to get an X-ray on my foot. I was on costly medication which wasn't helping. With a 5 minutes treatment the pain of the gout was better and a week down the line the gout got rapidly a lot better. Before the pain would cause tears. Now the pain has completely gone.

4. Recently I attended a transformational business conference in USA. I was struggling with post viral exhaustion and having difficulty integrating all that I learned into my daily life back home in London. Indigo's gracious presence stopped me in my tracks at a health shop in Balham. I felt such peace and reassurance after just five minutes of healing that I called her a few days later for a full session. During the session, I felt a stillness and vibrancy in my body that was beyond mere relaxation. I saw a clear vision of colourful fairy lights hanging in a beautiful outdoor party venue. People were dancing and singing together. It was made clear to me that the celebration was my future wedding. I am a divorced woman in my fifties. I have been content as a single woman for ten years. Clearly the Divine has a wicked sense of humour.

5. It was great to know you and talk about so many issues including religion and spiritualism. When you described what healing is about I was not sure that it would be really effective. Putting one's hand on the head did not sound like it would really deliver 'healing'. However, I was wrong. Very wrong. I felt something which I wish I could describe but peace would be one of them. Thanks Anthea and hope to have more healing sessions with you.

6. Thank you for your healing session on Wed. It was indeed my first and a divine experience. The session starts timely in the tidy room with a nice relaxing comfy chair. Anthea took enough time, till I got ready. She was a good listener and answered all the questions I had. After I felt very relaxed and sleepy. I felt my body, especially below my waist, heavier. I felt that, when I was walking back to the station, after I left your home. I thought this was one of my physical sensations. I could not go to bed early the day I acquired the session because I needed to go out after but I slept longer than usual yesterday and my body feels ok. Not sure how it will be unfolded from here but I am calmly excited.

7. I was delighted to get some healing from Anthea. She is a lovely lady and I felt extremely relaxed after our session. I also experienced a connection with my mother who died 6 years ago.

8. I am pretty much submerged in my spirit and spiritual pursuits and I'm a connector for others and Spirit, so I don't tend to look for people to help me make that connection myself, but when I met Anthea I felt that we had 'business' to take care of together. The session was marvellous for me, as it was really nice to just chill and have someone else direct the show, especially since at the time I was going through some life turbulence and was having issues connecting and getting my mind to quiet down for more than five seconds! What I loved the most was just the silence and even though my mind was still going on warp speed I was still able to connect with the Divine Beloved in me and around me. I had lots of experiences - angels turned up to say hi, issues that were bothering me were addressed and regarding my physical health, I was even handed a peace note. A whole host of imagery and sensations happened - and in the few weeks since, their meanings have unfolded in amazing ways but everything came in with a deep feeling of peace and of being held in grace, a feeling that I have had more ease reconnecting to on a daily basis since the session. Since the session, my still small voice within has become louder - making it easier to make decisions for myself on a daily basis that are about following my heart and doing what is best for me. The session also cranked up my synchronicity experiences and so it is much easier for me to find the things I need - I don't seem to have to search now, just acknowledge, everything is right there, simple and perfect for me, which is greatly encouraging. This has helped me become more mindful and peaceful, I don't spend forever trying to figure things out nor doubting the gift of the message that I've been given. I feel like the session most helped me with finding my place in the Universe again.

9. I received some healing from Anthea at a particularly challenging time in my life and was amazed just how beautiful the experience was. I immediately felt very calm and relaxed and started to regain a connection with my soul again which lasted for some time after the treatment! I would heartily recommend Anthea to anyone! Love and Light!

10. Thank you for the healing session yesterday. I felt so happy afterwards! It was a powerful experience. You really connected me to some positive powerful energy. On a physical level my congested sinuses/blocked head were completely cleared and I could breathe for the first time in months. There was also a clear message from Spirit encouraging me to be more grounded in my body, on the planet. I realise I have been denying my human body wishing only to function at the Soul/Spirit level. On a communication level, you helped me reconnect to my "Divine Line", my "team". I recently realised that "going it alone" is not workable and a strong, constant connection to Spirit is required if we are to truly be of service to the One, the Christ Consciousness. I was grateful to receive clear messages and guidance both regarding the states of my physical health and spiritual practice. Thank you for your gift of healing and support.

11. Anthea came to our home and following a lovely lunch and catch up offered a healing session to both my husband and I. The sessions were very relaxing and after she left we both fell into a deep sleep despite the early hour. We woke feeling refreshed and revitalized and later went on to have the best night's sleep. That would have been testament enough to her wonderful gift however there is more to be told. We had a lodger living with us who had a bad addiction problem and her heavy energy was beginning to really darken our living space and having an impact on us both. The plan was to ask her to move out but we never got the chance because less than a week after our treatments she left without a word. What a relief! I have no doubt that the two incidences were connected and I am thankful to Anthea for coming into our home and helping to re-establish a healthy and happy space. Life feels peaceful and harmonious once again! Thank you.

12. In the middle of the 5 mins I saw a strike of lightening. Also I felt little things passing through my skull. It felt very relaxing but my head felt very tense at the same time.

13. Hi good evening Anthea. What a wonderful experience I've had today. The session was 5 mins and worth every minute. I felt like my worries and stresses lifted up out of me and disappeared. There was peace and everything was calm. It was though everything just floated away. I have a slight problem with my stomach area, and I have an mri scan next Monday. As I was thinking about it I could feel something moving gently inside of my body and then float away. An awesome experience thank you.

14. I was shocked to find that Anthea's fingers were firmly placed between my crown and back of head as I felt as if I was being massaged on my forehead during the spiritual healing session. My head felt really heavy and then it felt really light, like it was empty. It was a very relaxing feeling and I felt quite lightheaded for the rest of the day.

15. I went to Anthea's spiritual healing session with an open mind. I closed my eyes and relaxed in the chair and she placed her hand on my head. During that time, I felt pulsating twitches on my head, which was interesting, considering Anthea's hand was stationery. After the session, I felt very relaxed and peaceful. I would highly recommend it.

16. It was an enormous blessing to attend Anthea's spiritual healing session in her lovely home. She provided the time and space for me to reflect on my life in a meaningful way and begin to articulate what could be God's purpose for my future. I came into the session with a headache, but my mind felt healing and I was filled with joy and peace by the time the session was finished - my headache had disappeared!! I urge anyone to try this. You will be amazed by how simple but effective it is for your life. Thank you again Anthea for sharing your gift with me.

17. Thank you for my first and ever spiritual healing session. It was very relaxing and the tension headache I was experiencing was elevated after my session which was wonderful.

18. I had a spiritual healing session with Anthea last week. I went to Anthea's home in North Acton where I was welcomed and greeted warmly by Anthea. Spiritual healing is not something I have done before and did not know what to expect during or after. Anthea and I chatted for a bit prior to laying her hands on my head and I closing my eyes for 5 minutes. During this time I felt I had a clear head and after the 5 minutes I felt completely relaxed. I discussed with Anthea I was seeking a new job and the next day I had an invite to attend a job interview. For the remainder of the day I felt relaxed and peaceful and slept really well on that night. I would very much recommend this experience to anyone.

19. As soon as she put her hand on my head, I felt like weight being lifted off my chest and felt hot afterwards. I came back for a second healing, after only 2 weeks of getting my first one because I felt I needed it. As soon as she put her hand on my head, I heard a voice say to me "Say what you want" and it was 100% not Anthea's voice. Then I started listing things I wanted, like; be a better person, be a better mum, be more patient with people, to be more peaceful and to be more loving towards everybody, things like that. Then after that my mind started wondering about random things and then I had a feeling that I cannot explain, like an out of body experience. I felt my first healing was a mind healing and a body healing. I felt today was a personality healing. My spirit was telling me I needed another healing. I am glad I did.

20. I went to visit Anthea in her cosy home in Acton. I felt a bit nervous to go at first but she made me feel very comfortable and welcomed. I had told her about some of the issues that had been bothering me lately. She placed her hands on my head and within minutes I felt a hot sensation coming from my lower abdominals, it almost felt like I had a ton of bricks on my chest and Anthea's hands were sucking the negative energy out. I began to cry and moments later I felt very calm. Afterwards my fingers and toes felt completely numb and for the rest of the day I felt light headed. I feel that the healing session was telling me to trust my instincts more and protect my energy and to not feel guilty about letting people who hurt me go! I highly recommend Anthea she has an amazing gift!

21. ..."We don't meet people by accident, they're meant to cross our path for a reason." I feel I'm at a special place in my spiritual journey and my encounter with Anthea was exactly what I needed at that moment to bring me here today. My session with Anthea was beautiful. I felt very present in my body and in those few moments it felt as if a portal of grace had opened and a precious gift was passed onto me. Later that night I felt a strong divine presence and had a dream in which I felt myself smiling. I feel I am a step closer to my truth. Eternally grateful to you. Love ❤...

22. It was a real joy to receive healing from Anthea just over a month ago. She had a lovely caring persona which immediately made me feel at ease. During the healing that lasted around 5 minutes, I felt a wonderful sense of calm and deep relaxation. At the end of the session I felt as though I was coming out of a profound and very deep meditation. This peaceful sensation transmuted into a wonderful sense of a calm and deep connection with my inner being, which lasted for some time. I would recommend Anthea to anyone who might be interested. Thank you Anthea for sharing this special gift of healing that you have been given!

23. The time we spent together on Sunday was like a release valve; which to my mind is 'healing'. Healing from the negative thoughts about relationships. Talking to you about it meant that I was able to process my thoughts and feelings in such a way that I could understand them better and move on with a more positive mindset. My mind needed that release. Can't thank you enough.

On opening her eyes, after the spiritual healing, she spoke about photos that she had seen of migration and war torn countries. She spoke of the risk of the photographers. She said she had wondered as a new photographer, could she take this risk herself. She said she had concluded that she would take photos that brought her peace. She spoke of taking up again, writing a journal to help her to look at her life's story so far, in particular to let go of resentment and forgive. She said her photos of peace would help her, to write this difficult journal. She said she did not like to confront others. As she spoke of her difficulty in confronting, I saw a vision of three images pass in front of me, like three rectangular holograms and was given a thought for each one. One image was the photos of war torn countries, one image was her photos of peace, one image was her difficulty in confronting others. I received understanding of their connection, that I was given; to feed back to her. That she would have to take the risk like the photographers of the war torn countries, to confront the people she needed to, to gain the peace she wanted, like her photos of peace. It was the first time, I had seen a vision whilst a person was talking, after their spiritual healing.

24. I went see Anthea a week ago, because I felt I was going through emotional turmoil. I was on edge and had been irritated for some time. I went looking for hope and answers. During my session I found it extremely hard to relax even though I thought I was relaxed, but when I did, I felt at peace. And although I feel like I'm still going through emotional turmoil I feel I am more in control. During the spiritual healing I experienced the following sensations: pulsating in my head, I saw the edge of a gold photo frame, I saw a baby, I saw the colours blue and purple.

25. I attended the spiritual healing service, out of curiosity and to see if it could help me. Anthea put her hand over my head, and I felt a sort of heaviness above my head, but I was still sceptical. Over time, I think it helped me in certain ways. My kids wanted this board game which cost £18 to £30. I didn't really want to buy it, but one lunch time, I said to myself "I'm going to buy this game today and really cheap". I went to a local charity shop, found the game straight away, hardly opened for £2. I went for regular walks with my mum, she had new boots and kept tripping over. One evening, I knew she was going to fall and told her so and then she tripped and fell over, luckily she wasn't hurt. Out of the blue, I met this lady and we ended up chatting for ages and had so much in common, even though we were from different communities (walks of life). I felt like she had been sent to me for a reason, to help me solve some of my issues with my kids. My son had hidden an item in his room. One day, I decided to look into his drawers, and noticed something unusual, I checked it and he had hidden an item he shouldn't have had. I thought to myself, I had no reason to check his room, but something made me do it on that day. These could all be coincidences, but I do think they happened for some reason.

26. I recently attended Anthea's spiritual healing sessions a few weeks ago after meeting her during a walking tour in East London! I've always been into personal growth and trying to identify different things that hold me back and trying to move forward with my life. I always aspire to be the best version of myself and when Anthea told me about her spiritual healing service I was naturally intrigued! So I went to one of her free 5 minute sessions in North Acton. I sat down in a chair and within about a minute I went into a deep relaxation. I felt something happen but didn't know exactly what. After the session was finished I went back home and felt compelled to do a 20 minute meditation. After a few minutes I felt a wave of energy surround me. It was a really strange experience but I felt connected to something higher. I believe that changes are starting to occur on a deep subconscious level now and this will help me with my personal growth going forward.

27. I've gone in to a very still place of Peace. It is most spacious and pleasant. Our last session was very very very still indeed. Particularly in comparison to the one before which was raucous and intense. A couple days after our session, I just dropped in to this Peace and am Being here Now.

28. I've been trying to find the words to say about today and I'm still so speechless. But I can't thank you enough. I literally feel so relaxed and calm with myself and it feels so amazing as I've felt so stressed with everything lately. Honestly feels like a weight has lifted off my shoulders. Literally no words to describe. Just thank you so much.

The following, A to E, are accounts of five different client experiences, written by me.

A. She explained after her session, that following a new job, she had been focusing on positive visualisations e.g., the law of attraction and abundance though from the universe, not from God, however during her session she heard a voice say, "I am the Universe". She also said the session left her feeling happy.

B. He asked me if I could heal his hand, as he had recently fallen in the snow and it had become injured. I explained, I could not determine what healing would take place for a client but that I would happily give him a session, if he would still like, which he said he would. After the session, as I do not know what has transpired in a client's healing session, unless a client chooses to tell me, I learnt that he had seen the faces of two friends who had been the source of much distress, however the faces had been configured to display what was in their hearts, so the face images reflected this. They showed fangs hanging from them. He then saw a huge angel come behind him and put his arms around him, as well as at the same time, hearing a voice repeating tenderly, "You have nothing to fear". He also said he felt an enormous feeling of love that had been given to him. When we spoke afterwards, he told me that he was a psychotherapist; had been trying to help these two friends, for some time but had received much unpleasantness from them. We spoke about the difficulty we face, when we over extend ourselves in an attempt to save someone, forgetting that we run into dangerous waters when we unwittingly assume an external role to save another person who is in tumult, not understanding that this is a call for them to turn within, as our Divine moral duty is to support others; to choose to save themselves. We also spoke about forgiveness; in particular, that a person who has caused you hurt but is refusing to seek your forgiveness is choosing to withhold care from you, so keeping company with them should not continue at this time, though you must not harness negative feelings within you towards them. He told me he had been pondering over this for the last couple of weeks and the session had brought him much needed clarity, insight and peace.

C. A client explained that during her second healing session, she had been reminded of her dream, which she had long forgotten, to open up a Healing/Retreat centre for people in need. She was working in the financial industry.

D. After the session she explained that, initially her mind was full of lots of thoughts, then it was like someone had put peace into it and for the first time in ages her mind was quiet. And she heard a voice repeating "Everything is going to be alright". She felt like a huge physical weight had been lifted from her and she felt like she had no worries and the day was going to be great. She also felt a tingling in her heart.

E. Before the session, he told me he could see a white aura circling above me. He is trained in Reiki. After the session, he told me that he had seen Jesus. I said to him that I was so glad, particularly as I had something to tell him. I told him that when he had shown me his book on 'archangels' before the session, as there is a mass of misinformation on 'angels/archangels' in books and on the internet, I wanted to tell him this Truth but was receiving Divine Wisdom from Jesus, not to do so. Though I was confused as to why, as Jesus had shown me this. However, as I revere the teachings, instruction and life guidance from Jesus, I refrained from doing so, surmising that he would arrive at this Truth in a perfect, Divinely cultivated and Divinely timed way for him. He then said to me, that he now knew why Jesus had placed his finger over His lips indicating 'shush' and that he had wondered at the time why Jesus had done this. When we spoke of our two separate experiences and realised how they fitted together, we were both astonished.

Printed in Great Britain
by Amazon